Sources in Late Antiquity and Byzantium

# Sources in Late Antiquity and Byzantium

## Leslie Kelly

**Westphalia Press**
An Imprint of the Policy Studies Organization
Washington, DC
2020

Sources in Late Antiquity and Byzantium
All Rights Reserved © 2020 by Policy Studies Organization

Westphalia Press
An imprint of Policy Studies Organization
1527 New Hampshire Ave., NW
Washington, D.C. 20036
info@ipsonet.org

ISBN: 978-1-63723-891-2

Cover and interior design by Jeffrey Barnes
jbarnesbook.design

Daniel Gutierrez-Sandoval, Executive Director
PSO and Westphalia Press

Updated material and comments on this edition
can be found at the Westphalia Press website:
www.westphaliapress.org

# Abstract

This book introduces the student of Late Antiquity and Byzantium to the types of literary sources they are most likely to encounter in their studies, explaining how these genres work, and noting peculiarities of each genre that the historian must take into account in order to utilize them as sources for history. Frequently encountered genres that carry over from Late Antiquity into Byzantium were selected for inclusion. The work is divided into the broad, sometimes overlapping, categories of panegyrics and *Lives*, legal and administrative texts, literary letter collections, and sermons. For each source type, a brief historical overview of the genre is provided, as is a discussion of its main characteristics. The function of these genres in Late Antique and Byzantine society is examined and examples are provided. This book does not break new ground, but rather seeks to provide a synthesis of current scholarly theories on these source types for easy consumption.

*To my Somerville friends*

## Table of Contents

Chapter 1: Introduction ............................................................. 1

Chapter 2: Praise and Emulation ............................................... 3

Chapter 3: Prohibition and Prescription .................................. 35

Chapter 4: Literary Letter Collections:
The Rhetorical and the Pragmatic ........................................... 65

Chapter 5: Admonition and Exhortation ................................. 85

Chapter 6: Conclusion ............................................................ 107

Translations ............................................................................ 109

Bibliography ........................................................................... 117

## CHAPTER 1
# Introduction

This book introduces the student of Late Antiquity and Byzantium to the types of literary sources they are most likely to encounter in their studies, explaining how these genres work and noting peculiarities of each genre that the historian must take into account in order to utilize them as sources for history. Frequently encountered genres that carry over from Late Antiquity into Byzantium were selected for inclusion. The work is divided into the following broad, sometimes overlapping, categories:

- Panegyrics and *Lives*
- Legal and administrative texts
- Literary letter collections
- Sermons

Each of these genres has classical or imperial predecessors, but there was a sharp increase in the production of these source types beginning in the fourth century CE, and their genre norms and social functions shifted. For each source type, a brief historical overview of the genre is provided, as is a discussion of its main characteristics. The function of these genres in Late Antique and Byzantine society is examined and examples are provided. This book does not break new ground, but rather seeks to provide a synthesis of current scholarly theories on these source types for easy consumption.

In Chapter 2, Praise and Emulation, we look closely at two types of praise material: speeches in praise of an emperor and biographies that celebrate the lives of holy men and women. These provide us a window into Late Antique imperial ideology and religion in Late Antiquity and Byzantium. In Chapter 3, Prohibition and Prescription, we examine texts designed to regulate, including imperial law codes, church orders, and monastic rules and foundation documents. We consider how these laws and regulations came to be and what they can tell us about actual political and religious concerns and practices and examine the function of both secular and ecclesiastical law in Late Antique and Byzantine societies. In Chapter 4, Literary Letter Collections: The Rhetorical and the Pragmatic, we see how the set structure of the letter allowed for versatility, examining its social, political, and religious uses. In Chapter 5, Admonition and Exhortation, we take up the steady stream of sermons that were preached to Late Antique and Byzantine Christians on a weekly basis, categorizing and analyzing them to determine the types of information they may yield.

A survey of these source types, so prevalent in daily life, can teach us much about Late Antique and Byzantine society. In learning the roadmap that ancient authors followed and the expectations of their target audiences, we are provided with an insider view of their world.

CHAPTER 2

# Praise and Emulation

I begin this chapter with a "big picture" overview of the role that public praise played in Late Antique and Byzantine societies. Elaborate, public praise was worked into the fabric of political, social, and religious life in Late Antiquity and Byzantium. Starting at the top of the social pyramid, the emperor was a focus of regular, public praise speeches. His subjects praised God (or the gods) for his benevolent rule and thanked him for his many benefactions. Cities sent ambassadors to hail a new emperor's reign or to seek and receive benefits, and individuals might also praise and thank him for appointment to an office. Imperial visits to cities were also an occasion for speeches of praise. Below the emperor, imperial administrators were offered public speeches of praise and thanks on similar occasions. In the church, bishops or lay patrons of the congregation were publicly praised, and these could be living or deceased. And then there was the veneration of the saints, which took place throughout the year, with numerous services in the liturgical calendar designated to commemorate their exemplary piety. Then too, there is the place of praise in the lives of regular, ordinary individuals. People gave speeches to honor their cities, to honor their families; there were also speeches of praise for special occasions such as birthdays, weddings, or funerals. Taking all these occasions together then, and thinking of the number of government officials, the number of congregations, and the number of persons celebrating life events, we can see that speeches of praise were a constant, pervasive feature of Late Antique and Byzantine culture.

Consequently, it is no surprise that many types of works in both periods involved praise including the two genres that we take up in detail in this chapter, imperial panegyrics and the *Lives* of saints. Because, as is shown below, there were some standard features to the way that praise was bestowed, there is significant overlap in the conventions of each, and characteristics of both of these genres can also be identified in other genres of the time in which praise played a natural part. For example, in a letter of recommendation, the fourth-century CE rhetorician Libanius praises the family, education, and character of the youth Faustinus in ways strikingly similar to the pattern and style of an orator delivering a panegyric on an emperor or governor or of a disciple writing about a saint (B77).[1] The historian Ammianus Marcellinus includes a panegyric section on the emperor Julian in his Roman history, which provides a good example of the style and content of imperial panegyric, although it occurs in this Late Antique work of history:

> Urged on by his [Julian's] native energy, he dreamed of the din of battle and the slaughter of savages, already preparing to gather up the broken fragments of the province, if only fortune should at last aid him with her favouring breeze. Accordingly, since the great deeds that he had the courage and good fortune to perform in Gaul surpass many valiant achievements of the ancients, I shall describe them one by one in progressive order, endeavouring to put in play all the resources of my modest ability, if only they will suffice. Now whatever I shall tell (and no wordy deceit adorns my tale, but untrammelled faithfulness to fact, based upon clear proofs, com-

---

1   Letter B77 is translated by Scott Bradbury, *Selected Letters of Libanius from the Age of Constantius and Julian* (Liverpool: Liverpool University Press, 2004), 114–15 (where Bradbury's numbering system, with the designation "B" is utilized). Most of the translations in this work are taken from standard series, such as the Loeb Classical Library, *Nicene and Post-Nicene Fathers,* Fathers of the Church, or the New City Press translation of the works of Augustine. Full information for these translations is provided in the bibliography. Where these are not available, or where an alternative reading was preferred, a footnote with full translation information is provided at the first point of use, with a shorthand note for any subsequent citations. For the sake of convenience, brief primary sources are included in parenthetical notes within the body of the text.

## CHAPTER 2: PRAISE AND EMULATION

poses it) will almost belong to the domain of the panegyric. (Ammianus Marcellinus 16.1-3)[2]

Having established the larger context for the function of praise in Late Antiquity and Byzantium, we seek now to move on to the specific regulations that governed where, when, and how praise was bestowed. What follows next is a brief description of the rules or conventions governing the practice of praise, which provides context for our focused discussion of imperial panegyrics and saints' *Lives*, two genres that were characteristic of these two periods.

Let us start with the vocabulary and a survey of the ancient texts that explicitly discuss the characteristics or desired features of panegyrics. The Greek and Latin words for panegyric are *panegyrikos* and *panegyricus*, respectively. Panegyric was part of a larger category of epideictic or display oratory (*genus demonstrativum* in Latin).[3] The ancient Greeks gave speeches to celebrate athletes, cities, individuals who had died (in funeral speeches), and living rulers.[4] Aristotle included epideictic in his fourth-century BCE manual, *Rhetoric*; another fourth-century BCE text, *Rhetoric to Alexander* (*Rhetorica ad Alexandrum*) discusses it as well. Moving on to the Romans, discussions in early Roman works include *Rhetoric for Herennius* (*Rhetorica ad Herennium*),

---

2   C.E.V. Nixon, "Latin Panegyric in the Tetrarchic and Constantinian Period," in *Latin Panegyric*, ed. Roger Rees (Oxford: Oxford University Press, 2012), 223 notes Ammianus Marcellinus's use of panegyric; on the relationship between history and panegyric, see Alan J. Ross, "Libanius the Historian? Praise and Presentation of the Past in *Or*. 59," *Greek, Roman, and Byzantine Studies* 56 (2016): 293–320.

3   C.E.V. Nixon and Barbara Saylor Rodgers, "General Introduction," in *In Praise of Later Roman Emperors*: *The* Panegyrici Latini. *Introduction, Translation and Historical Commentary*, eds. C.E.V. Nixon and Barbara Saylor Rodgers (Berkeley: University of California Press, 1994), 1–2.

4   D.A. Russell and N.G. Wilson, eds. and trans., *Menander Rhetor* (Oxford: Oxford University Press, 1981), xiii–xxxiv trace the trajectory of this speech type and discuss its relationship to related forms.

dating from the late first-century BCE, and there are scattered references in the works of Cicero and in Quintilian, *The Orator's Education* 3.7 (first century CE). Aelius Theon, a Greek sophist in the first or second century CE, included epideictic in his collection of exercises in composition, *Progymnasmata*. References to epideictic appear during the Second Sophistic in the works of Alexander of Numenius and Hermogenes of Tarsus.

Two works produced in the late third century CE and attributed to Menander Rhetor and Pseudo-Dionysios are perhaps the most important for scholars today, as these deal with the subject at length.[5] The work of Menander Rhetor is taken up more fully below. The date of Pseudo-Dionysios, *On Epideictic Speeches*, is contested, but it likely dates to the same period as that of Menander (from the same time as Treatise II attributed to Menander, on which see below).[6] It takes up panegyrics for festivals, marriage speeches, bridal chamber speeches, birthday speeches, welcoming speeches to incoming governors, funeral speeches, and exhortations to athletes.[7] In the late fourth and early fifth centuries CE, Nicolaus of Myra and Aphthonius also produced *Progymnasmata*, which continued to be read into the Byzantine era.

Handbooks of style dating from the Second Sophistic and from Late Antiquity were also still in use in the Byzantine period and commentaries on these were produced.[8] New handbooks of rhetoric were created as well as *Progymnasmata*.[9] The evidence suggests that there may have been periods when there were fewer opportunities for speeches specifically in imperial circles, but

---

5   Russell and Wilson, *Menander Rhetor*, xl.
6   Russell and Wilson, *Menander Rhetor*, 363.
7   A translation of this text is included in Russell and Wilson's appendix.
8   Elizabeth Jeffreys, "Rhetoric in Byzantium," in *Companion to Greek Rhetoric*, ed. Ian Worthington (Malden, MA: Wiley-Blackwell, 2010), 170–71; Elizabeth Jeffreys, "Rhetoric," in *The Oxford Handbook of Byzantine Studies*, eds. Elizabeth Jeffries, John F. Haldon, and Robin Cormack (Oxford: Oxford University Press, 2008), 829–30.
9   Jeffreys, "Rhetoric in Byzantium," 172–77; Jeffreys, "Rhetoric," 829–30.

the *Book of Ceremonies* (tenth century CE) and *Treatise on the Dignities and Offices* (fourteenth century CE) suggest occasions when they would have been appropriate and we do have scattered extant examples.[10] Beginning in the sixth century, speeches before an emperor began to include advice in addition to praise.[11] Imperial speeches of the Byzantine period also reflect the theocratic nature of the state: the emperor is praised as God's earthly representative.[12] Private speeches pick up after the eleventh century and there were speeches to personal patrons, wedding speeches, and funeral orations.[13]

As we can see then, there was a long tradition of the use of panegyric and in developing rules for how to do it properly. We now turn to the explanation and description of epideictic speech associated with Menander Rhetor. The level of detail provided in the treatises associated with Menander on epideictic speech makes it worthwhile to devote serious attention to them, and then too, even though we know that other handbooks, which are no longer extant, were also in circulation, we can see the rules that Rhetor lays out reflected in numerous writings, including imperial panegyrics and *Lives*.

---

10 For contrasting views on this issue, see Jeffreys, "Rhetoric in Byzantium"; Jeffreys, "Rhetoric"; Anthony Kaldellis, "The Discontinuous History of Imperial Panegyric in Byzantium and its Reinvention by Michael Psellos," *Greek, Roman, and Byzantine Studies* 59 (2019): 693–713, which addresses the gap from 640 to 1040 CE and the reinvigoration of epideictic oratory at the imperial court under Michael Psellos.

11 Jeffreys, "Rhetoric in Byzantium," 174; Jeffreys, "Rhetoric," 832–33; for thirteenth century developments, see Dimiter G. Angelov, "Byzantine Imperial Panegyric as Advice Literature (1204-c. 1350)," in *Rhetoric in Byzantium: Papers from the Thirty-Fifth Spring Symposium of Byzantine Studies, Exeter College, University of Oxford, March 2001*, ed. Elizabeth Jeffreys (Aldershot, UK: Ashgate, 2003), 55–72; in contrast to Late Antique speeches, see Nixon and Rodgers, "General Introduction," 23.

12 G.T. Dennis, "Imperial Panegyric: Rhetoric and Reality," in *Byzantine Court Culture from 829 to 1204*, ed. Henry Maguire (Washington, DC: Dumbarton Oaks Research Library and Collection, 1997), 135.

13 Jeffreys, "Rhetoric in Byzantium," 172–73.

Two treatises on epideictic speech attributed to Menander of Laodicea-on-Lycus, commonly known as Menander Rhetor, were combined into one in antiquity and in this form they have come down to us. Neither treatise is complete. Based on the number of differences between them, it is likely that they are by two different authors rather than by the same author but written at two different times. The attribution of the (combined) work to the reign of Diocletian is based on historical references in the treatises.[14] Treatise I begins with public speeches of praise and blame (1.1.2). Speeches of praise are divided into those for gods (hymns) and those for mortal objects. This second category is divided further into praise of cities and countries and praise of living creatures (1.1.3). Menander describes how to praise countries, cities, harbors, gulfs, or an acropolis. Menander stresses the need to dress up bland facts, gloss over the bad, and turn any potential negatives into a positive. "If the city's location should be completely devoid of things to praise … then we must incorporate that very thing into our praise on the grounds that the inhabitants are thereby compelled to be philosophical and tough" (1.11.4). If one is praising an emperor and his lineage is not prestigious, start with the emperor himself (2.1.9). These tactics are used in all types of panegyrics, biographies, and hagiographies throughout the Late Antique and Byzantine periods.

Menander describes speeches in honor of gods and festivals, and speeches of arrival and departure for public officials and for private individuals. Incoming governors should be greeted with elaborate praise and thanksgiving (2.2). When a scholar is about to leave his hometown for university, he may deliver a farewell speech (2.14). There are wedding speeches and funeral speeches, birthday speeches, and speeches of consolation. There are speeches made to the emperor. These may include requests on behalf of a city (2.12).

---

14   Russell and Wilson, *Menander Rhetor,* xxxvi–xl.

Because of the adoption of its talking points across genres, it is especially fruitful to study the characteristics of imperial orations, speeches of praise to an emperor, or, in the Greek phrase, *basilikos logos*.[15] The emperor is to be praised for such things as are generally understood, by common consent, to be good (2.1.1). The basic points covered in such a speech are:

- the emperor's city or nation and then his family and his birth
- his wonderful nature and education
- the emperor's accomplishments and then actions (that is, actions in times of war and actions in times of peace)
- association of his actions to various virtues (courage, justice, temperance, or wisdom)
- the emperor's fortune or fate
- comparisons to previous reigns
- a conclusion that provides a positive evaluation of his reign.

The features in this list are readily identifiable in both the extant praise speeches for Roman emperors and in the hagiographical accounts of the saints. Let us turn now to a discussion of those genres.

## Imperial Panegyrics

As shown above, the evidence of the style handbooks makes it clear that there were numerous occasions for public speeches of praise in Late Antiquity.[16] These were not the same occasions

---

15   On this, Laurent Pernot, *Epideictic Rhetoric: Questioning the Stakes of Ancient Praise* (Austin, TX: University of Texas Press, 2015), 31 writes, "The second treatise attributed to Menander Rhetor provides the best guide for studying the *topoi* for the encomia of persons. Its first two chapters ... offer a full list, intended for the encomium of an emperor."

16   Nixon and Rodgers, "General Introduction," 3 note that although few have survived, there must have been a steady deluge of such speeches delivered around the empire.

as would have occurred under the Roman Republic or during the Early to High Empire. According to Pernot, "Major political oratory ... in the traditional sense of vital questions, such as wars, alliances, taxes, etc. ... no longer existed."[17] Rather, by Late Antiquity, a new type of epideictic had developed in its place.[18] This new epideictic was wielded before emperors and governors, assuring the imperial center of provincial and personal loyalty and affirming the authority and legitimate rule of the state.[19] Apart from state occasions, as noted above, there were domestic celebrations, and patrons to thank. Whether official or private, praise speeches were a common way to confer honor.[20] Delivering a good speech reflected well on both subject and orator.

Let us look at some examples of imperial panegyrics from the Latin West and the Greek East. In what follows, it will be seen that imperial panegyrics were in broad lines extremely similar, took up the same themes, and often followed a similar structure. Another feature that strikes the modern reader is that they are also full of hyperbolic statements with excessive, and at times downright outrageous, praise of the emperor. But it is our aim to see the reason behind these conventions. It is the system of imperial panegyric that we must understand: why did this system, with its particular set of conventions, its narrow set of rules for content and structure, develop in the first place, and what function did it serve?

We begin with Late Antique Latin speeches. Latin imperial panegyrics survive in a collection of twelve speeches called the *Panegyrici Latini* (abbreviated in what follows as *PL*).[21] These

---

17  Pernot, *Epideictic Rhetoric*, 13.
18  Pernot, *Epideictic Rhetoric*, 67.
19  On imperial ceremonies as a vital part of the relationship between emperor and subject, see Sabine G. MacCormack, *Art and Ceremony in Late Antiquity* (Berkeley: University of California, Press, 1981).
20  Pernot, *Epideictic Rhetoric*, 91-92.
21  For other examples of Latin panegyric beyond the *PL*, see Roger Rees, "The Modern History of Latin Panegyric," in *Latin Panegyric*, ed. Roger Rees (Oxford, Oxford University Press, 2012), 7.

were composed between 289 and 389 CE for various occasions, such as to celebrate military victories, the anniversaries of imperial offices, or to offer expressions of thanksgiving to the emperor (for being appointed to a consulship or on behalf of a city for tax relief). The first one in the collection is an early speech, delivered in 100 CE by Pliny the Younger, in which he gave thanks to Trajan for the opportunity to serve as consul. This was evidently taken as a model, and the other eleven are from authors who had a connection to Gaul.[22] The *PL* as a collection is thought to have been designed to provide models for the youth of Gaul, young men intending to enter into public office.[23] They provide practical models for the mechanics of the political system and also serve to imbue students with proper political attitudes.[24] This then is a partial answer to the question of purpose and function for this particular set of panegyrics. Other pertinent facts are that the *PL* were contemporary and were not revised for publication.[25] For this reason they are sometimes the best evidence for individual events from this time period. But at the same time, the *PL* were selected to provide good examples of style and rhetoric rather than being selected on the basis of their historical content; also, having been produced in the West, they hardly mention eastern emperors at all.[26] Furthermore, despite the fact that they were later made into a collection, at their original point of delivery, they were not intended to be a lasting possession, but were speeches given once and not distributed for widespread reading across the empire.[27]

---

22  Nixon and Rodgers, "General Introduction," 4; Roger Rees, *Layers of Loyalty in Latin Panegyric, AD 289–307* (Oxford: Oxford University Press, 2002), 22.

23  Nixon and Rodgers, "General Introduction," 31–33; for date and authorship, see 3–10 and 26–33.

24  Nixon, "Latin Panegyric," 237–39.

25  Nixon and Rodgers, "General Introduction," 33; Nixon, "Latin Panegyric," 237; compare Dennis, "Imperial Panegyric," 137 on Byzantine-era imperial panegyrics.

26  Nixon and Rodgers, "General Introduction," 34.

27  Brian Warmington, "Aspects of Constantinian Propaganda in the *Pane-*

Thus far, the potential yield of this source type for the historian appears limited. But this is misleading! There is much that they can teach us about political and religious history. By examining the forms and themes of these speeches and by comparing them to the rules laid out in Menander Rhetor's handbooks and to other examples of imperial speeches, we can make inferences about imperial perception and reception of imperial ideology.

To start with, we can learn about the mechanics of imperial public relations. They turn out to be subtler than one would have guessed upon first reading the sort of fulsome complements woven throughout the *PL*. As has been ably demonstrated by Nixon, these speeches cannot be considered to represent imperial propaganda as there is no evidence of the speakers having been pre-selected by the imperial court to speak and the speakers were not in active office when they spoke.[28] However, the *PL* could still be said to reflect imperial wishes due to the fact that they were part of the educational system in Gaul, which itself was supported by imperial patronage.[29] And certainly we can see that the orators would take care to say things congenial to their emperor. For example in *PL* III(11).6-9, a speech to Julian, the speaker describes Emperor Julian's journey to the East in the wake of his acclamation as emperor by the troops as a peaceful venture

---

*gyrici Latini*," in *Latin Panegyric*, ed. Roger Rees (Oxford, Oxford University Press, 2012), 336.

28 C.E.V. Nixon, "Constantinus Oriens Imperator: Propaganda and Panegyric. On Reading Panegyric 7 (307)," *Historia: Zeitschrift für Alte Geschichte 42.2 (1993)*: 229–46; Nixon, "Latin Panegyric," 228–38. There is at least one instance in which it appears likely that the orator in question had in fact been primed. This is when an anonymous panegyrist claims descent from Claudius Gothicus for Constantine, and hence that he ruled by hereditary right, see *PL* VI(7).2.2; discussed in Nixon, "Latin Panegyric," 233 and C.E.V. Nixon, "*Panegyric of Constantine* by an Anonymous Orator (310)," in *In Praise of Later Roman Emperors: The Panegyrici Latini. Introduction, Translation and Historical Commentary*, eds. C.E.V. Nixon and Barbara Saylor Rodgers (Berkeley: University of California Press, 1994), 220 n.6.

29 Nixon, "Latin Panegyric," 235–36.

that brought about much needed corrections to that area—rather than depicting it as a journey to confront Constantius, which would have been a more accurate, though less palatable, description.[30] He also contrasts Julian's austere lifestyle, a trait on which Julian prided himself, with the wasteful habits of other emperors (*PL* III(11).10.3 and 11.4). When looked at as a whole, we can conclude that the orators designed their speeches to be pleasing to imperial ears, but that they were not given specific directives.

Bearing witness to the occasional, concrete event is not the only thing that we look for in a historical source. MacCormack suggests that panegyrics help us to appreciate the worldview of the speaker. The panegyrist was "trained by his culture" to perceive and interpret events in a certain way.[31] Similarly, Pernot writes of the "common language" of the speeches, an analysis of which can help us to better understand "the horizon of expectation" of both speakers and audiences.[32] In these speeches, then, we can perceive the values of Late Antiquity.[33] The *PL* provide good information on imperial ideology—how the emperor was perceived, how he wished to be perceived, and how he related to his subjects and to the divine.[34]

Late Antique values can be identified by careful examination of the rhetorical techniques that the orators consciously employed

---

30   Discussed in Samuel N.C. Lieu, ed., *The Emperor Julian: Panegyric and Polemic: Claudius Mamertinus, John Chrysostom, Ephrem the Syrian* (Liverpool: Liverpool University Press, 1986), 17 n.15. The numbering of the *PL* follows that used in Rees, *Layers of Loyalty*, 20. The Roman numeral in the primary source citation denotes the sequence of the speech within the collection; the Arabic numeral denotes its chronological order.

31   MacCormack, *Art and Ceremony*, 26.

32   Pernot, *Epideictic Rhetoric,* 62.

33   Pernot, *Epideictic Rhetoric*, 94–100.

34   For events, see Rees, "Modern History," 33 and Dennis, "Imperial Panegyric," 137–39 (for Byzantine-era examples); on religion and ideology, see Rees, "Modern History," 36–38; Rees, *Layers of Loyalty,* 21; MacCormack, *Art and Ceremony*, 8–14.

in these speeches.³⁵ Some common devices were apostrophe, hyperbole, comparison, and metaphor.³⁶ Hyperbole is perhaps the one that first strikes the modern historian. Pernot writes, "Hyperbole, by its very definition, serves to amplify or diminish: in this way, it coincides with the aims traditionally assigned to praise and to blame, and is particularly suited to the epideictic genre."³⁷ But Quintilian tells us that there were limits. "It [hyperbole] means an elegant straining of the truth, and may be employed indifferently for exaggeration or attenuation .... But even here a certain proportion must be observed. For although every hyperbole involves the incredible, it must not go too far in this direction, which provides the easiest road to extravagant affectation" (*The Orator's Education* 8.6.67 and 73). As Pernot puts it, "Hyperbole is a lie, but not a lie intended to deceive."³⁸ In other words, it was not the case that "anything goes" when it came to exaggeration; there were rules. Both the speaker and the audience were familiar with these rules and would know how to interpret hyperbole when they heard it. We should think of our Late Antique target audience as discriminating, rather than credulous, and the orators of the *PL* as skilled writers, working hard within the confines of a narrow tradition to produce an effect of novelty, rather than as sycophants of limited abilities.

The subject of the address could be present but did not have to be. At the very least, the subject was, however, a real person, and the known facts about him or her could act as a check on the speaker.³⁹ Dennis, on Byzantine-era panegyrics writes, "People

---

35   Technical effects are discussed by Nixon and Rodgers, "General Introduction," 19–21.
36   Pernot, *Epideictic Rhetoric,* 57–61.
37   Pernot, *Epideictic Rhetoric,* 59.
38   Pernot, *Epideictic Rhetoric,* 60.
39   Tomas Hägg and Philip Rousseau, "Introduction: Biography and Panegyric," in *Greek Biography and Panegyric in Late Antiquity,* eds. Tomas Hägg and Philip Rousseau (Berkeley: University of California Press, 2000), 14–15.

## CHAPTER 2: PRAISE AND EMULATION

in the audience had participated in those events, and the orator, while permitting himself some embellishment, could not present a total fabrication."[40]

The themes mentioned in the handbook of Menander Rhetor are identifiable in the *PL*. But the orators of the *PL* did not follow the guidelines of handbooks slavishly and may have had access to other handbooks that influenced them. Panegyrists could leave some traditional themes out or they might choose to highlight specific ones. It was very common for a speaker to downplay his own ability to speak, a common practice of literary authors as well (see for example Julian, *To Empress Eusebia* 106a; 126b). Speakers would often depict the emperor as having assumed his duties only out of a sense of obligation or dire necessity.[41] This was part of imperial ideology and the mark of good emperor. (The same held true for bishops). For example, in *PL* VII(6).1.1, Maximian is said to have returned to the imperial throne reluctantly, only out of necessity, "for ever Augustus, whether you will it or not."[42] Maximian had returned to power after having abdicated with Diocletian, and his panegyrist takes pain to portray him as having reluctantly returned from retirement, having been compelled by the people and the gods to assume power once more. Another example (mentioned above) would be when Claudius Mamertinus, in a panegyric thanking Julian for appointing him consul, presents Julian's march to the East as being inspired by a wish to revitalize the empire. "All of these problems, however, finally wore down the resolute and unyielding patience of the greatest of princes" (*PL* III(11).6).[43]

---

40  Dennis, "Imperial Panegyric," 127.

41  On the theme of reluctant emperors, see MacCormack, *Art and Ceremony*, 199; as a philosophical ideal, see Susanna Elm, *Sons of Hellenism, Fathers of the Church: Emperor Julian, Gregory of Nazianzus, and the Vision of Rome* (Berkeley: University of California, 2012), 74.

42  Translated by Rees, *Layers of Loyalty*, 177; discussed 176–77.

43  Translated by Marna M. Morgan in Lieu, *The Emperor Julian*, 17.

We have been examining Latin speeches, but several examples of Greek imperial panegyric have also survived from antiquity. Emperor Julian composed three Greek panegyrics, two to Constantius and one to Constantius's wife, the empress Eusebia. The orator Libanius has several panegyrics of this type; there are also imperial panegyrics by Greek Church Fathers. Eusebius, Bishop of Caesarea, for example, produced two panegyrics on the occasion of Constantine's Thirtieth Jubilee, which have come down to us as one combined work, the *Triennial Oration* or *De laudibus Constantini*.[44] In all of these speeches, Greek or Latin, we see certain themes repeating, so that we can pick out what we might call imperial predilections for epithets and motifs. So, although we are in a sense drawing a negative conclusion by stating that these speeches were not utilized as a delivery service for imperial messages, this fact in itself tells us something about the informal nature of imperial messaging. Elite orators clearly took an active role in this informal "system" as willing participants in first shaping and then adhering to a set of rules governing the way to deliver imperial praise.

In the case of Julian, it is even possible to see a future emperor himself playing this game and in the process, revealing the persona he would one day project to the empire. In reading the panegyrics of Julian with the conventions of the genre in mind, one can see how he skillfully employs but also deviates from them so that his own personality is unmistakably stamped onto them. Julian's *Speech of Thanks to the Empress Eusebia* has been analyzed in this way by Shaun Tougher, who demonstrates that this speech gives us a self-image of Julian, of his political situation as Caesar, and his intellectual bent.[45] I end this section of the chapter by demonstrating the way that knowledge of the genre allows

---

44   H.A. Drake, *In Praise of Constantine: A Historical Study and New Translation of Eusebius' Tricennial Orations* (Berkeley: University of California Press, 1976), 31–45.

45   Shaun Tougher, "In Praise of an Empress: Julian's *Speech of Thanks* to Eusebia," in *The Propaganda of Power: The Role of Panegyric in Late Antiquity*, ed. Mary Whitby (Leiden: Brill, 1998), 105.

us insight into the thought-world of Julian, and what this in turn tells us about the role of panegyrics in his society.

To set the stage, some brief context for the speech: Julian was Caesar in Gaul 355–361 CE. He was the last in the family line of Constantine. His half-brother Gallus was made Caesar in 351 but was suspected of treason and executed in 354. Julian was saved from a similar fate by the intervention of the empress and sent to Athens to study (*Oration* 3.118). He was recalled and appointed Caesar in 355, again with the intervention of the empress (Julian, *Orations* 3.121; Ammianus Marcellinus 15.8.3; Zosimus 3.1.2–3). As was commonplace, Julian speaks of the empress's native land (106c–107d) and praises the empress for her noble birth (107d–109a). But then he deviates from the standard format as, in praising Eusebia, he speaks primarily of her husband the emperor, saying that her primary virtue is that she has engendered a high regard for herself on the part of Constantius, and he spends a fair amount of time praising Constantius in the speech (112b–114c; see also 109b–110a; 114b–c). But in the end, Tougher concludes that the panegyric is much more about Julian himself than about either Constantius or Eusebia, as can be seen from the fact that he uses the speech to contrast his own austere and philosophical lifestyle with that of the empress.[46] Eusebia is described by Julian as being fond of luxury (110d–112b; 129b–d); Julian was a lover of books, one who "delighted in literature," philosophy, and learning (118c–119a; 120b–c; 121d; 123d–125a; 125d–126b), and was decidedly anti-pomp (121d).

Julian wanted to be celebrated as a philosopher. His writings, including this panegyric for the empress, make that clear. Orators were careful to praise these traits: Claudius Mamertinus praised Julian for that in *PL* III(11).10.3; 11.4. In a speech in honor of the consulship of Emperor Julian, assumed on January 1, 363 CE, Libanius praised the emperor for his intellectual, philosophical, and religious training:

---

46  Tougher, "In Praise of an Empress," 121.

[H]e set himself to acquire something more noble than empire—philosophy and eloquence. Such, Sire, is my verdict, and I have learnt it from you who prefer the possessions of learning to the provinces you govern Observing rhetoric to be a means of persuading the masses whereas philosophy induces knowledge of matters more exalted, he thought it improper to discourse adequately on the one subject and yet show an ignorance of higher things. So he combined both studies and made an amalgam of them, elevating his intellect by a study of heavenly lore and at the same time, by his association with rhetoric, training his tongue to run trippingly. (Libanius, *Oration* 12.29-30; see also 32; 54-55; 92, 94-95)

We can see in Julian's panegyric for Empress Eusebia that he cannot help but insert his own agenda even into what should be a simple expression of thanks. In 121d, Julian discusses the need to use learning and philosophy properly. This was a regular theme of Julian's throughout his writings and one we see reflected particularly clearly in his exchange of letters with the orator Themistius. The correspondence between Themistius and Julian, which takes up the proper relationship between philosophy and power, allows us to better appreciate the undertones of Julian's speech of thanksgiving to the empress.

Themistius had written a letter to Julian after he had become Caesar, exhorting him to take up the life of the active philosopher (as Themistius himself had done at the behest of Emperor Constantius). No doubt this was intended as a compliment from one philosopher to another. But Julian's response, sent after he became Augustus, was negative. He accuses Themistius, and his now-deceased patron, Constantius, of having misunderstood the nature of the true philosopher and the best type of rule. For Julian a true philosopher meant someone who was wholly

## CHAPTER 2: PRAISE AND EMULATION

dedicated to the life of the mind and soul—he might advise a ruler but should not assume office himself (263c–266c). The best type of rule for a state to have is not an absolute monarch, but rather a man of extraordinary natural abilities who has so steeped himself in philosophy that his character approaches the divine (260d). Julian's ideas were not always clear—they were often out of synch with his contemporaries—but he seems in this letter to be wanting to combine both of these ideals, the philosopher-advisor and the semi-divine king, in the person of one super-human individual: himself. Susanna Elm, who has made a study of the political, religious, and philosophical thought of Julian, which includes a close reading of this particular letter, describes his outlook thus:

> Only a true philosopher, whether as emperor or as an emperor's advisor, could achieve the purity necessary to comprehend the divine to the degree possible for humans. Only such a figure could mediate appropriately between the divine and the rest of mankind, and therefore only he, either as emperor, public official, or advisor to those in office, could guide all in the manner appropriate to guarantee Rome's continued well-being.[47]

In expressing such sentiments, Julian was participating in a long-standing debate over the participation of the philosopher in active political life, which went back to ancient Greece and was once again a contested issue in Late Antiquity.[48] Philosophers were divided over whether they should take an active part in public life and as noted, Themistius himself had had to answer many critics due to his decision to assume a public office. For his part, Julian seems to want to have it both ways in this letter: he

---

47  Elm, *Sons of Hellenism*, 3.
48  Elm, 90–106. The philosophical context of the letter exchange is also discussed in Simon Swain, *Themistius, Julian, and Greek Political Theory under Rome: Texts, Translations, and Studies of Four Key Works* (Cam-

describes at length the very high standards that exist for both philosophers and rulers and states several times that he feels himself quite inadequate to assume office, loving philosophy as he does but having yet to attain complete enlightenment. If one took his arguments at face value, Julian seems to be arguing that is impossible for one to ever truly be a good philosopher or a good king. He himself, although devoted to philosophy, had certainly not yet achieved the highest levels of enlightenment. Consequently, he accepted the office of emperor only with the most extreme reluctance, as would any man who truly understood what it takes to be a good ruler, one steeped in philosophy and connected to the divine (253a; 258c; 259b; 260d; 266c–d). And yet Julian ends the letter with the clear indication that he believes he may in fact after all become this mythical philosopher-king, albeit with divine assistance:

> But should it be that blessings greater than of my furnishing and than the opinion that I now have of myself should be granted to men by God through my instrumentality, you must not resent my words. For being conscious of no good thing in me, save this only, that I do not even think that I possess the highest talent, and indeed have naturally none, I cry aloud and testify that you must not expect great things of me, but must entrust everything to God. (267a-b)

Julian's self-perception seems to have remained fairly constant, and the examination of his panegyric to the empress shows that he had already adopted this self-image early in his career. The evidence of his experiences with the genre, those composed by him and those composed in his honor, also shows us how central the genre of panegyric was in shaping the public perception of the emperor.

---

bridge, UK: Cambridge University Press, 2013), 53–91.

CHAPTER 2: PRAISE AND EMULATION

## *Lives*

We turn now in the second half of this chapter to a study of *Lives*. Biographies of holy persons, literary portraits of idealized types, began to be produced in the days of the early Roman empire and to proliferate in Late Antiquity and Byzantium. As demonstrated by Graham Anderson, the development of this genre was a product of the existence of real holy men and women, or individuals perceived as such, who fulfilled an important social need from the time of roughly the first century CE, through Late Antiquity, when such individuals took on an even greater importance, and into Byzantium.[49] The sudden increase in celebratory biographies of philosophers and saints reflects this historical rise of the holy man. Holy men and women of Late Antique and Byzantine society provided their communities with religious guidance. They served as patrons, mediating with the powerful on behalf of cities, villages, and individuals. Through healings and miracles (or at least through tales of their miraculous feats), they also brought the divine into the lives of ordinary people. Anderson writes:

> The root cause of the similarities between Byzantine hagiography and the holy men of the Empire is not just a matter of continuity of tradition; the social needs and conditions had not changed radically at grass roots level. Without any changes in the popular outlook on the physiology of disease, or the phenomenology of weather, it will still be attributed to demons and the saint will be credited with the removal of toxicity; without any increased understanding of the physical world he will be credited with ending droughts and earthquakes or the confinement of rivers.[50]

---

49  Graham Anderson, *Sage, Saint and Sophist: Holy Men and Their Associates in the Early Roman Empire* (New York: Routledge, 1994), 198–206.

50  Anderson, *Sage, Saint and Sophist,* 204–05.

This explains the continuity in the genre from the early empire to Byzantium, although each age also had its own unique concerns, some of which impacted the development of the *Lives*. Late Antiquity may be described as a period of intense religious rivalry and change. It was a time when religious experts of all types, including philosophers, were working out a new set of ideals. Such an atmosphere produced a new outpouring of *Lives* in Late Antiquity by both pagans and Christians. Pagans wrote *Lives* of philosophers and Christians wrote *Lives* of saints.

Biography of course did not originate in Late Antiquity. Biographical portraits had already developed in the Classical period.[51] Xenophon's *Agesilaus* was the first biography to resemble a Late Antique *Life* (as his *Memoirs* on Socrates did not include a chronological overview of the great philosopher). Like the *Lives* from the fourth century CE and beyond, *Agesilaus* included a description of the life and, as it may be phrased, the "way of life" of the Spartan king.[52] Skipping ahead to the Roman period, during the Second Sophistic, Philostratus wrote the *Life of Apollonius of Tyana*, a philosopher and holy man who was active in the second half of the first century CE. Apollonius of Tyana himself had written a biography of the ancient philosopher Pythagoras (c. 570–c. 495 CE), the founder of Pythagoreanism, as did two Neoplatonic admirers of Pythagoras, Porphyry (c. 234–c. 305 CE) and Iamblicus (c. 245–c. 325 CE).[53] Porphyry also wrote a *Life of Plotinus*, the founder of Neoplatonism and his teacher. Eunapius (346–c. 414 CE) published a collection of twenty-three philosophers and sophists (*Lives of the Philosophers and Sophists*).

The Christian development of the genre might be said to have started with the writings of the New Testament, in the gospel accounts of Jesus and in the Book of Acts, which records the

---

51  On the origins of biography and the development of biographical material in eulogies, see Hägg and Rousseau, "Introduction," 2–13.

52  Hägg and Rousseau, "Introduction," 3–4.

53  Anderson, *Sage, Saint and Sophist*, 12.

first generation of Christian followers. In the second century CE, Apocryphal Acts began to appear, with further narratives of the apostles. Eusebius included a biographical sketch of the Alexandrian church father Origen in Book 6 of his *Church History* and produced a biography of the first Christian emperor, Constantine. The *Life of Antony* is the earliest saint's *Life* proper. This was a fourth-century CE product and there was a solid output of individual saints' *Lives* from this time through the Byzantine period. Collections of saints' *Lives* also were popular: Jerome authored *Lives of Illustrious Men*, Rufinus authored *History of the Monks of Egypt*, and Theodoret of Cyrrhus authored *History of the Monks of Syria*.

In the Byzantine period, pre-existing saints' *Lives* continued to be read. New compositions were also produced, although at an uneven rate. The second period of the iconoclasm controversy was a high point of production (800s CE), as were the thirteenth and fourteenth centuries.[54] In the ninth and tenth centuries, *Lives* were created at the behest of patrons and tended to reflect their individual interests.[55] Compared to the periods before and after, there was a decline in the production of new hagiographies in the eleventh and twelfth centuries, although the eleventh century saw the development of new types of collections of hagiographical material.[56]

---

54  Alice-Mary Talbot, "Hagiography," in *The Oxford Handbook of Byzantine Studies*, eds. Elizabeth Jeffries, John F. Haldon, and Robin Cormack (Oxford: Oxford University Press, 2008), 866–67.

55  Stephanos Efthymiadis, "The Byzantine Hagiographer and His Audience in the Ninth and Tenth Centuries," in *Metaphrasis: Redactions and Audiences in Middle Byzantine Hagiography*, ed. Christian Høgel (Oslo: The Research Council of Norway, 1996), 65–69.

56  Symeon A. Paschalidis, "The Hagiography of the Eleventh and Twelfth Centuries," in *Ashgate Research Companion to Byzantine Hagiography. Volume I: Periods and Places*, ed. Stephanos Efthymiadis (Farnham; Burlington, VT: Ashgate, 2011), 143–71; for new collection types, see 144–47. On the gender imbalance in Byzantine era hagiographies of the Middle and Late Byzantine periods, see Alice-Mary Talbot, "General Introduction," in *Holy Women of Byzantium: Ten Saints' Lives in English*

Late Antique and Byzantine *Lives*, our present focus, whether as standalone texts or as part of a collection, followed a predictable pattern: the philosopher or saint lives a life of great purity and holiness and as such is instrumental in converting others to his or her way of life.[57] The protagonists, or heroes of the story, often perform healings and miracles. *Lives* were essentially narratives of "revelation"; they were intended to reveal how the human and the divine meet, and to demonstrate how the hero partakes of divine nature.[58] The author uses the biographical account to showcase a set of ideals or values in the hopes that his readers will imitate those values into their own lives. Why so many *Lives* at this time? Above, it was noted that the proliferation of *Lives* in Late Antiquity was a product of the religious atmosphere of the age, a time marked by competing systems of thought, pagan and Christian. But within each of these divisions, there were also innumerable subdivisions. It is not quite correct therefore to speak of "philosophical ideals" or "Christian ideals" since there was no one agreed upon doctrine, practice, or way of life among pagan or Christian communities. The increased production in Late Antique pagan and Christian *Lives* should consequently be understood not only as a response to external, competing models of life, but also as a response to internal critics within each

---

*Translation*, ed. Alice-Mary Talbot (Washington, DC: Dumbarton Oaks Research Library and Collection, 1996), x–xiv.

57 In a set of collected lives, the author would use each individual life in his collection to illustrate the same set of ideals. On this, see Patricia Cox Miller, "Strategies of Representation in Collective Biography: Constructing the Subject as Holy," in *Greek Biography and Panegyric in Late Antiquity*, eds. Tomas Hägg and Philip Rousseau (Berkeley: University of California Press, 2000), 221. Gregory of Tours, in the preface to this *Life of the Fathers*, writes: "it is better to speak of the 'Life of the Fathers' rather than, 'Lives of the Fathers,' the more so since there is a diversity of merits and virtues among them, but the one life of the body sustains them all in this world": translated by Edward James, *Gregory of Tours: Life of the Fathers*, 2nd ed. (Liverpool: Liverpool University Press, 1991), 2.

58 Patricia Cox, *Biography in Late Antiquity: A Quest for the Holy Man* (Berkeley: University of California Press, 1983), 13; 132.

respective tradition. The authors of these biographies were taking part, sometimes a contentious part, in a larger discourse that was both internal and external.[59]

As an illustration of dueling idealized portraits, we turn to the work of Eusebius. Eusebius's biographical works can in part be seen as a response to the growing body of pagan literature that presented a model for the philosophical life.[60] For example, Porphyry's *Life of Pythagoras* depicts the philosopher having many of the same traits as the saints in Christian *Lives*: like them, Pythagoras can tame animals and nature, foretell the future, and perform miracles. Porphyry had attacked Christianity at length in his own writings and Eusebius was keenly aware of this, responding to individual statements attributed to Porphyry in several of his publications.

Book 6 of Eusebius's *Church History* contains a biographical sketch of the Alexandrian church father, Origen. Eusebius makes plain that this biographical sketch is intended as an apology or defense of Origen. Eusebius had in fact already written a formal *Apology* for Origen and that work served as the basis for the description of the life and work of Origen found in Book 6. Both were written in response to Christians who did not approve of Origen's theology.[61] "The elder brethren among us have handed down many other facts respecting Origen which I think proper to omit, as not pertaining to this work. But whatever it has seemed necessary to record about him can be found in the Apology in his behalf written by us and Pamphilus, the holy martyr of our day. We prepared this carefully and did the work jointly on account of faultfinders" (6.33.4). But Patricia Cox

---

59  The combative literary atmosphere in which biography flourished is explored in Cox, *Biography in Late Antiquity*, passim; see also Miller, "Strategies of Representation," 209–54.

60  Cox, *Biography in Late Antiquity*, 139–41, with respect to his biographical sketch of Origen.

61  Cox, *Biography in Late Antiquity*, 136–39.

has demonstrated that Eusebius's portrait of Origen was at the same time directed outward, as a response to pagan criticisms. His description of Origen has many parallels to Porphyry's *Life of Plotinus*—too many, given his familiarity with the writings of Porphyry, to be a coincidence.[62] In *Church History* 6.19.2–11, Eusebius quotes a passage from Porphyry's work in which the philosopher denigrates Origen, where part of the accusation against Origen is that he and other Christians misunderstand the plain sense of the Mosaic Law and try to read it in an inappropriately philosophical fashion: "For they boast that the plain words of Moses are enigmas, and regard them as oracles full of hidden mysteries; and having bewildered the mental judgment by folly, they make their explanations" (Eusebius, *Church History* 6.19.4). Eusebius's biographical sketch of Origen attempts to answer both Christian critics and pagan critics; he presents Origen as the perfect blend of both the Hellenic, philosophical "divine" and the new, Christian theologian.[63]

The biographies of Pythagoras and Plotinus composed by Porphyry and Iamblichus can also to be understood as looking both

---

62 Cox, *Biography in Late Antiquity*, 34; 36–38; 40–41; 139–41.

63 Cox, *Biography in Late Antiquity*, 70–71. Eusebius even seems to have had Porphyry in mind when he crafted his depiction of the first Christian emperor. In *Life of Constantine*, Eusebius presents Constantine as a saintly ruler, a true Christian king, but also as a second Moses. The *Life of Constantine* begins with an explicit comparison between Constantine and Moses in 1.12 and includes several telling parallels throughout: 1.19–20, 27–29, 32; 4.75; Constantine as Moses in the *Life* is discussed in Averil Cameron, *Christianity and the Rhetoric of Empire: The Development of Christian Discourse* (Berkeley: University of California Press, 1992), 55; 145; Averil Cameron, "Form and Meaning: The *Vita Constantini* and the *Vita Antonii*," in *Greek Biography and Panegyric in Late Antiquity*, eds. Tomas Hägg and Philip Rousseau (Berkeley: University of California Press, 2000), 75. Porphyry had argued that Israelite religion was actually derived from the Phoenician religion: Anthony Meredith, "Porphyry and Julian Against the Christians," *ANRW* II. 23, no. 2: 1132. Since Moses was the lawgiver of the Israelites, in making this argument, Porphyry had essentially "claimed Moses for the pagan side": Cameron, "Form and Meaning," 74.

## CHAPTER 2: PRAISE AND EMULATION

outward at Christian groups and inward at competing pagan constructions of philosophical ideals.[64] Their biographies "can be read both as apologetic efforts to maintain allegiance to the pagan standard and as political manifestos, justifications of pagan supremacy based on the virtues inherent in its tradition and hallowed figureheads."[65]

We turn now in the last section of this chapter to a more in-depth examination of saints' *Lives*. Their number and circulation speak to their popularity. Saints' *Lives* were intended to have and did have a wide circulation.[66] They were written to be sent out to the wider world.[67] Admiration but also emulation was the desired goal, as the authors themselves tell us.

> *He Who fashioned* our *hearts alone, Who understands all* our *works*, as the holy Scripture says, and Who foresees the instability of our minds and how our thoughts tend toward evil things from our youth, has consented in His goodness that contemporary authors should set down in writing the lives, the deeds of contest and asceticism, and the extraordinary and most marvelous achievements of the saints who lived before the law, under the law and in the time of grace,—I mean those of the

---

64  Cox, *Biography in Late Antiquity*, 142–45; Gillian Clark, "Philosophic Lives and the Philosophic Life: Porphyry and Iamblichus," in *Greek Biography and Panegyric in Late Antiquity*, eds. Tomas Hägg and Philip Rousseau (Berkeley: University of California Press, 2000), 29–51.

65  Cox, *Biography in Late Antiquity*, 145.

66  On the "textual mobility" of *Lives*, see Hägg and Rousseau, "Introduction," 17; for concrete examples of the circulation of saints' *Lives* and their impact in one Egyptian village, see T.G. Wilfong, *Women of Jeme: Lives in a Coptic Town in Late Antique Egypt* (Ann Arbor, MI: University of Michigan Press, 2002), 21–45.

67  Stephanos Efthymiadis and Nikos Kalogeras, "Audience, Language and Patronage in Byzantine Hagiography," in *Ashgate Research Companion to Byzantine Hagiography*. Vol. 2: *Genres and Contexts*, ed. Stephanos Efthymiadis (Farnham, UK/Burlington, VT: Ashgate, 2014), 253.

prophets, apostles, martyrs, and blessed ones. <Such authors have> left <their accounts> like living icons or clean and very clear mirrors for subsequent <generations> in order that when, as the Apostle says, we *consider* their lives and *their behavior* through these <stories>, we *may follow their faith*, and in order that whatever path someone desires to travel he may do this easily and without stumbling, finding his guide therein. For nothing leads so naturally toward the way of virtue or, on the other hand, is so good at making <people> despise all transitory things, whether these bring sorrow or joy, as when <an account of> a life which is virtuous and pleasing to God falls on the ears of those who love Him. (Gregory the Cellarer, *Life of St. Lazaros* 1)[68]

The subject matter of a *Life* might be a fierce ascetic who had limited contact with the world, but his story was to be read and heard by all the faithful: by those living in cities and in villages, clergy and laypersons, married and unmarried.[69] What was to be imitated were the virtues exhibited by the saint, not necessarily the milieu of the saint. The reader of the *Life of Antony* was not expected to renounce the world and move to the desert, but rather to emulate the saint's traits in his or her own sphere.[70] As Hägg and Rousseau write, "usefulness governed belief: people were willing to believe what they found useful; willing to welcome a model that would reinforce behavior they already valued."[71]

---

68   The italics indicate biblical phrases; translated by Richard P.H. Greenfield, *The Life of Lazaros of Mt. Galesion: An Eleventh-Century Pillar Saint* (Washington, DC: Dumbarton Oaks Research Library and Collection, 2000), 75.

69   Lynda L. Coon, *Sacred Fictions: Holy Women and Hagiography in Late Antiquity* (Philadelphia: University of Pennsylvania Press, 1997), 152; Hägg and Rousseau, "Introduction," 16–17; for spread in villages, see Wilfong, *Women of Jeme*, 21–45.

70   Hägg and Rousseau, "Introduction," 17; 21.

71   Hägg and Rousseau, "Introduction," 19.

## CHAPTER 2: PRAISE AND EMULATION

Characteristics of saints' *Lives* are fairly uniform. The saint commonly

- exhibits great piety and learning in childhood
- excels at learning in adulthood
- is a wonderful, effective teacher of religious truths
- lives an usually austere and hardworking life, exhibiting great feats of ascetism, such as not eating for extended periods of time; braving the elements; or working harder, longer, or better than others
- helps the oppressed
- mediates disputes
- offers spiritual guidance
- combats heresy and paganism
- heals
- performs miracles, controlling nature and animals
- prophesies
- battles demons and
- expresses a reluctance to court fame, to see visitors, or to assume official duties (such as becoming head of a monastery or being appointed bishop).

The overlap between this list and Menander Rhetor's guide to praising an emperor (his education, his accomplishments, his virtues) is readily apparent. This list is not exhaustive and not every *Life* included all tropes. Some themes only appeared in the Byzantine period. In the fifth through the ninth centuries CE, a recurring motif was the female monastic who lived disguised as a male monk (Mary/Marinos, Anastasia/Anastasios, Matron/Babylas, or Anna/Euphemianos, for example). There were thirteen such in this period.[72] The iconoclasm controversy

---

72 Vasileios *Marinis*, "The *Vita of St. Anna/Euphemianos*. Introduction, Translation, and Commentary," *Journal of Modern Hellenism* 27–28

was reflected in *Lives* produced during both phases of the conflict (with production in the second phase outpacing that of the first), and there was an increased interest in apocalyptic motifs in the tenth and eleventh centuries and an increased use of classical language in *Lives* in the twelfth century.[73]

Let us consider some Byzantine examples in which we can clearly identify the tropes. The *Life of Anna/Euphemianos* dates from the first half of the ninth century CE. The *Life* opens with a contrast between the wicked iconoclast emperor and the blessed Constantine and Irene. The *Life* depicts a saint who was originally married, but once her husband and children died, she gave away all of her wealth to the poor and entered a monastery (as a man), where she performed miracles. Her reputation resulted in so many converts to the monastic lifestyle that the monastery became overcrowded and a new location had to be established.

The *Life and Conduct of Our Holy Mother Irene Abbess of the Convent of Chrysobalanton* (976–1025 CE) overtly celebrates the end of iconoclasm and commemorates the imperial women who helped bring this about, and in Section 4, there is a brief mention of the "tyranny of the Iconoclasts." But the usual *topoi* are still the main structural elements of the *Life*: her life as abbess is foretold by a holy man (3), she studies the Scriptures and the *Lives* of the Fathers fervently (5; 6), her asceticism is beyond that of her peers (5; 16), she is tempted by the Devil and attacked by demons (6; 11), she accepts leadership of the convent only with great reluctance (7), she teaches her fellow nuns and all those who come to the monastery (8; 10), she has the gift of prophecy (9; 12; 22), she sees visions (13), she heals the possessed (15), she displays miraculous powers (16; 21), and she performs posthumous miracles (24).

---

(2009–2010): 53.

73 Talbot, "Hagiography," 866; Paschalidis, "The Hagiography of the Eleventh and Twelfth Centuries," 157. For more themes and categorization of periods, see Efthymiadis, *Ashgate Research Companion to Byzantine Hagiography*. Vols. I–II.

## CHAPTER 2: PRAISE AND EMULATION

Gregory the Cellarer, a disciple of the eleventh century pillar-saint Lazaros, wrote a *Life* of the saint not long after his death in 1053 CE and other versions were to follow. The saint lived on a pillar at St. Marina, near Ephesus, for seven years and then moved onto the mountain of Galesion. He attracted many visitors. A number of monasteries grew up around him. The *Life* begins with his place of origin and his parents, followed by a miraculous birth (2); he was unusually pious, charitable, and studious as a child (3–4); his asceticism surpassed that of other men (10; 17; 35; 53; 59; 81–82; 111–12); he turned heretics to orthodoxy (10); he had the gift of prophecy (13; 78–79; 88–110; 221; 223; 227); he helped those in need (7; 8; 15; 32; 36; 145–46; 248) and mediated disputes (122); he became a priest only with extreme reluctance (17), striving always to avoid fame (72; 74; 78; 145); he tamed wild animals and scorpions (22; 55) and others were able to control bears and goats by invoking his name and his blessing (64; 77); he battled demons (54-56; 58-59; 67–69; 81); he performed healings, exorcisms, and other miracles of various types (70–71; 73–76; 159; 211–14; 236; 243); and he was known for his wonderful teaching (123; 128; 147).[74]

Gregory of Constantinople, *Life of St. Romylos*, a fourteenth-century text begins with a statement of the desire to inspire emulation (1), then dives right into the noble origins of the saint, the famous city of Vidin, and his pious parents (2). His superiority was made known even in childhood as he was admired not only by his peers, but also by his teacher (2). He earned a glowing reputation for his humbleness and his assiduous attentions to the sick (5). The saint wrestles with demons (12), is an especially effective teacher (15–17), and performs posthumous miracles (24).

What is the value of these saints' *Lives* for historical research? Lynda Coon has examined in some detail the influence of biblical

---

74   Examples of his teaching are interspersed throughout (see, e.g., 180–96). Other monks in this narrative also battle demons (42–52; 166–67; 174; 218; 244), give to the poor (161), and practice an extreme asceticism (159; 162; 164–65; 168; 171–73).

types or models on the development of these saintly tropes. She argues that these characteristics and activities were selected for inclusion in the *Lives* because they represented biblical ideals—rather than being in any sense a true historical record.[75] It is just as likely, however, that there was mutual influence between the reality on the ground and the development of the conventions of the genre, a dynamic that we can identify in comparable situations from antiquity. James Goehring, among others, has noted the impact of the stories of desert ascetics on the development of subsequent communities of desert monastics, describing it as a self-perpetuating system.[76] But we can also find corroboration in a comparison with other source types. To take but one example, saints' *Lives* often depict the saint as helping the oppressed. Papyrological evidence provides corroboration. Lincoln Blumell and Thomas Wayment, in their study of Christian Oxyrhynchus, note that a letter found at Oxyrhynchus, from one Theon to Pascentius, may actually have been composed by the Theon mentioned in Rufinus's *History of the Monks of Egypt* (166).[77] This holy man was highly educated, knowing Greek, Latin, and Coptic, and lived near Oxyrhynchus in the late fourth or

---

75   Coon, *Sacred Fictions*, 28–51. Coon also argues that the tropes are entirely male-oriented, having been selected by male authors who shaped the *Lives* of holy women from top to bottom and that it is only the (masculine-oriented) theological message of the *Lives* that we can find in them. She writes: "In short, all saints' lives are rhetorical, didactic, and constructed. They are sacred fictions, not factual accounts of human achievements.... These texts allow the historian to reconstruct the perspective of the male authors rather than the historical reality of the women whose stories are recounted" (xxi).

76   James E. Goehring, "The Encroaching Desert: Literary Production and Ascetic Space in Early Christian Egypt," *Journal of Early Christian Studies* 1, no. 3 (1993): 281–96; repr. in Goehring, *Ascetics, Society, and the Desert: Studies in Early Egyptian Monasticism* (Harrisburg, PA: Trinity Press, 1999), 73–88. See also Cameron, *Christianity*, 57, who summarizes it nicely: "Written *Lives* were mimetic; real ascetic discipline in turn imitated the written *Lives*."

77   Lincoln H. Blumell and Thomas A. Wayment, eds., *Christian Oxyrhynchus: Texts, Documents, and Sources* (Waco, TX: Baylor University Press, 2015), no. 156, 585–89.

early fifth century CE. A bilingual letter, written in Greek and Latin, dating to that time, from Theon to Pascentius, requests Pascentius's assistance on behalf of a petitioner. Theon writes, "Wherefore, the old woman came and asked for letters for your inspired opinion: she recounted, 'I am being wronged and they are wronging my son.' And so assuredly know that if there is any justice in her, please devoutly assist her" (*POxy* 28.2193).

This chapter has been devoted to an exploration of works of praise. We have seen that broadly speaking, imperial panegyrics and saints' *Lives* had their origins in the praise culture of Late Antiquity and that both were shaped by the guidance laid out in Menander Rhetor's handbook for how to deliver praise properly. Emperors and saints belonged to the realm of power in their own right, both being perceived as super-human, and both also further served as mediators between the common person and the supernatural. Individually, these genres are sources for imperial and religious ideology, showing us the thought-world of the people of Late Antiquity and Byzantium and how they perceived their connection to their government, their Deity, and their faith community.

CHAPTER 3

# Prohibition and Prescription

In this chapter, we consider legal and administrative texts, including Roman and Byzantine law codes and novels, ecclesiastical law or canons, church manuals or handbooks, monastic rules, and *typika* or monastic foundation documents. All of these different sources are dealt with in this one chapter because, although they each tend to have more than one purpose, they each have in common that at least one of their purposes is to explain what rules are to be followed and/or what penalties will ensue for those who do not adhere to them. Moreover, the way that we as students of history need to approach them is similar. These genres can easily lead the unsuspecting to project an idealized situation of universal compliance that does not reflect lived reality. Christian prescriptions and proscriptions, for instance, were often framed in universal terms, but this does not necessarily mean that they were enforced across the entire Christian community, or even that they were intended to be. Imperial law codes have for the most part come down to us encased in the language of officialdom that would seem to leave no room for non-conformity. But as is shown below, a law, even an imperial decree, could not be universally enforced. It is always necessary therefore, when working with these materials, to keep in mind that the texts give us what was desired, and sometimes only what was desired by a small group of people, rather than what was necessarily happening on the ground across an entire empire. In what follows, we focus on two methods of approach to these texts: the straightforward, when the law itself contains hints of why it was enacted or the problem it attempts to address, and comparison and contrast with other sets of rules, whether from the same period and/or community or between periods or groups.

## Imperial Law Codes and Novels

As we turn to the imperial law codes of Late Antiquity and Byzantium, it behooves us to first pause and consider how the individual laws that make up these codes came to be. Although it is an oversimplification, it is still fair to say that during the Early and High Roman Empire, laws were created in a reactive way, that is, as responses to problems encountered on the ground or as responses to petitions, and that this carried through into the Late Antique period.[78] "A *suggestio*, proposal, from the official backed by a report was the most common means of supplying information from below and prompting an imperial decision."[79] Tony Honoré explains the process: a suggestion for a new law was put forward and came to the consistory, that is, the heads of the bureaus or *scrinia*, who may at that point add necessary background information to the proposal before sending it on to the *quaestor*, the official in charge of drafting the laws; the proposed law then traveled to the consistory again for consideration and the *quaestor* then created the final version.[80] In 446 CE, the senate was made part of the

---

78   Caroline Humfress, "Law in Practice," in *A Companion to Late Antiquity*, ed. Philip Rousseau (Malden, MA: Wiley-Blackwell, 2009), 390.

79   Jill Harries, "Introduction: The Background to the Code," in *The Theodosian Code: Studies in the Imperial Law of Late Antiquity*, eds. Jill Harries and Ian Wood (Ithaca, NY: Cornell University Press, 1993), 8.

80   Tony Honoré, "The Making of the Theodosian Code," *Zeitschrift der Savigny-Stiftung für Rechtsgeschichte. Romanistische Abteilung* 103 (1986): 137–39; Tony Honoré, "Some Quaestors of the Reign of Theodosius II," in *The Theodosian Code: Studies in the Imperial Law of Late Antiquity*, eds. Jill Harries and Ian Wood (Ithaca, NY: Cornell University Press, 1993), 74. For more on the process, see Jill Harries, *Law and Empire in Late Antiquity* (Cambridge: Cambridge University Press, 1999), 36–53; John Matthews, *Laying Down the Law: A Study of the Theodosian Code* (New Haven: Yale University Press, 2000). We can see evidence in tenth- and eleventh-century laws for the roles of petitioners and of officials in stimulating a law or in helping compose it: Marie Theres Fögen, "Legislation in Byzantium: A Political and a Bureaucratic Technique," in *Law and Society in Byzantium*,

process and any new general law had to be discussed and approved by them (*CJ* 1.14.8).[81] The imperial center then sent out the law to the provinces and officials there made their own copies and set up public notices.[82]

Before turning to the individual codes, we must also note some common characteristics and themes that run through all of the codes. One of the first things that one notices when reading the imperial law codes is the amount of repetition in them. This could be taken as evidence that the laws were ineffective so that the government was forever having to republish them in a vain attempt to ensure compliance. But Jill Harries, who has published extensively on law codes in Late Antiquity, warns against this easy assumption. The system of Roman law was set up with the premise that Roman emperors and governors would reissue laws when they came into power. The reiteration of the same laws again and again reassured people that the law was the same as it had been for a predecessor.[83] It was an effort on the part of the state to ensure that the law was clear and as such should rather be seen as proof of the efficacy of law rather than an indication of its inefficiency. Repeated laws were therefore laws that actually worked.[84] In a somewhat similar vein, Late Antique law codes and the surviving records of trials often refer to corruption. But it was not necessarily the case that judges were becoming more corrupt in the post-Diocletian era. Rather, we can see such accusations as proof of the fact that citizens were confident that

---

*Ninth-Twelfth Centuries*, eds. Angeliki E. Laiou and Dieter Simon (Washington, DC: Dumbarton Oaks Research Library and Collection, 1994), 62–63.

81  *CJ* = Justinian's *Codex*

82  John Matthews, "The Making of the Text," in *The Theodosian Code: Studies in the Imperial Law of Late Antiquity*, eds. Jill Harries and Ian Wood (Ithaca, NY: Cornell University Press, 1993), 42; for a more detailed discussion, see Matthews, *Laying Down the Law*, 171–95.

83  Harries, "Introduction," 15; Harries, *Law and Empire*, 82–84; 87.

84  Harries, *Law and Empire*, 212.

once identified, corruption would be addressed; in other words, it was worth their while to speak out.[85]

The relationships among justice, the rule of law, and the emperor were part of the mix of Late Antique and Byzantine imperial ideology. The emperor was considered to be the ultimate enforcer of law in the Roman and Byzantine empires, but more than this, a good emperor must be a lover of justice. Menander Rhetor recommended praising an emperor for this very thing (2.1.27-31). "You should also say something about his lawmaking. 'He is a just lawmaker. He rescinds unjust laws and decrees just ones himself'" (2.1.31). An eighth-century legal text describes emperors as being "pious and justice loving" (*Krisis peri gambrōn stratiōtōn* 3–4).[86] In the ninth-century CE code, the *Eisagoge* the law is said to come "not just from any emperors, but from emperors who are especially remembered and celebrated for their orthodoxy and justice" (proem, lines 45-46).[87]

According to the imperial law codes, the emperor was not only the ultimate enforcer of law but also its ultimate source. In the constitution that commissioned Tribonian to begin the *Digest*, the emperor Justinian declared that the work of its authors should be considered as imperial constitutions, as if they were the words of the emperor, "for we ascribe everything to ourselves, since it is from us that all their authority is derived" (*Dig. Const. Deo Auctore* 6, 530 CE).[88] Such autocratic language permeates Late Antique and Byzantine imperial law codes. But

---

85   Harries, *Law and Empire*, 118–19.

86   Translated in M.T.G. Humphreys, *Law, Power, and Imperial Ideology in the Iconoclast Era: c. 680–850* (Oxford: Oxford University Press, 2015), 136.

87   Translated by W.J. Aerts et al., "The Prooimion of the Eisagoge," *Subseciva Groningana: Studies in Roman and Byzantine Law* 7 (2001): 99.

88   Translated by Alan Watson, "The Composition of the *Digest*," in *The Digest of Justinian: Volume I* (Philadelphia: University of Pennsylvania, 1985).

CHAPTER 3: PROHIBITION AND PRESCRIPTION

Roman emperors were not in practice the sole source of law and they were not able to enforce it without the consent of the governed. The stimulus for laws often came from the outside in, from provincial governors who became aware of problems on the ground in their regions or from special interests groups.[89] Roman emperors consulted advisors, lawyers, and officials when they made laws, and the drafting and approval of law was handled by a chain of persons.[90] Moreover, emperors did not have the manpower to ensure enforcement of all laws everywhere in the empire and the degree of local enforcement could vary, as it did for instance during the Great Persecution when Christians were pursued with unequal fervor.[91] So while imperial statements about the law and justice may be part of the "language of power" (to quote Harries), it was also part of the emperor's proof that he ruled by the universal consent of the people.[92]

Beyond the emperor's interest in justice and the rule of law, there are other recurring themes in the law codes, and these are often found in the proem or preface to each new code. In these opening statements, the reason for making the new code would be laid out, its origin-story, if you will, would be provided, and its contents and intended usage would be described. Imperial novels (*Novellae*), that is, decrees issued apart from the code, were also sometimes used for this purpose. Novels addressed issues that had been overlooked in the codes, that were not quite clear, or that had arisen since the latest code was published.[93] Proems

---

89   Harries, *Law and Empire*, 36; 49; 52.
90   Honoré, "Some Quaestors," 69.
91   Harries, *Law and Empire*, 96; Christopher Kelly, *Ruling the Later Roman Empire* (Cambridge, MA: Harvard University Press, 2004), 203–31.
92   Harries, *Law and Empire*, 97; see also 41; 58–59.
93   On the novels, see Bernard Stolte, "Justice: Legal Literature," in *The Oxford Handbook of Byzantine Studies*, eds. Elizabeth Jeffries, John F. Haldon, and Robin Cormack (Oxford: Oxford University Press, 2008), 693; on novels in the age of Justinian, see Caroline Humfress, "Law and

and novels show a desire for clarity and simplicity in the law, a desire that the law code be useful, and an emphasis on the role of Providence (that is, that the law was God-given, coming to human society via a God-ordained emperor). There is also a clear interest in one-upmanship. Each emperor who published a new code presented his project as the best that had ever been produced and in some cases would even refer to earlier codes in overtly derogatory terms. For example, the proem to the eighth-century law CE code known as the *Ecloga* states that "the laws enacted by previous Emperors have been written in many books and ... the sense thereof is to some difficult to understand, and to others absolutely unintelligible."[94]

Turning now to an overview of the major law codes from Late Antiquity and Byzantium, we begin with the Theodosian Code. The Theodosian Code, produced under Theodosius II (401–450 CE), was to be a collection of all the imperial laws from the time of Constantine up to his own reign which had general application (*CTh* 1.1.5).[95] Theodosius's *Novel* of 438 CE explains that he intended to make the existing overwhelming mass of laws more lucid and less obscure, to bring to them "the light of brevity."[96]

---

Legal Practice in the Age of Justinian," in *The Cambridge Companion to the Age of Justinian*, ed. Michael Maas (Cambridge: Cambridge University Press, 2005), 173–74); as responses to remaining problem areas in the newly revised codes (such as Justinian's *Novel* 60 of the year 537 CE), see Humfress, "Law and Legal Practice," 175.

94 Edwin Hanson Freshfield, *Roman Law in the Later Roman Empire: The Isaurian Period, Eighth Century, the* Ecloga (Cambridge: Bowes & Bowes, 1932), 39; see also the proem to the *Eisagoge* discussed below.

95 *CTh* = Theodosian Code. Theodosius also planned to produce another manual of law, but this did not happen: Matthews, *Laying Down the Law*, 10. Imperial pronouncements took different forms and not all of them had general applicability (see 16–19). On the types of laws issued in Late Antiquity (rescripts, edicts, etc.), see Harries, *Law and Empire*, 20–35.

96 All translations of this work are taken from Clyde Pharr, *The Theodosian Code and Novels, and the Sirmondian Constitutions: A Translation with*

CHAPTER 3: PROHIBITION AND PRESCRIPTION

But another reason may also be discerned. The code refers to the unity of the empire (*CTh* 1.1.5) and the relationship between Theodosius and his western counterpart, Valentinian III, is surely relevant. In 437 CE, Eudoxia, the daughter of the emperor of eastern half of the empire, Theodosius II, had married the emperor of the West, Valentinian III. This marriage symbolized a unified empire, but Theodosius was senior. He had been responsible for restoring the throne in the West to Valentinian (or rather, to his mother, Galla Placidia). In producing the code, Theodosius took charge of the legal system and appropriated one of the key duties of an emperor to himself alone; the code may thus be seen as an assertion of precedence over the younger emperor.[97]

*CTh* 1.1.5 and 1.1.6 give us some indications of the processes of collecting and editing that were to be used by the commission entrusted with the project. Above, we outlined the stages that a law went through before it was collected into the Code. The law as it appears to us today in the Theodosian Code may include wording from any of these stages.[98] Due to the way the laws were promulgated, laws existed in different versions across the empire. Honoré writes, "It was natural for the government to adapt the text of the law to the addressee, in order to stress points of special concern to him."[99] John Matthews has demonstrated that some of the laws included in the Theodosian Code were

---

*Commentary, Glossary, and Bibliography* by Clyde Pharr, in collaboration with Theresa Sherrer Davidson and Mary Brown Pharr; with an introduction by C. Dickerman Williams (Princeton, NJ: Princeton University Press, 1952). Pharr's translation is sometimes problematic, but it is sufficient for our present purposes.

97  Honoré, "Making of the Theodosian Code," 176–81; for fuller discussion of the circumstances behind the compilation of the Code, see Matthews, *Laying Down the Law*, 1–54.

98  Honoré, "Making of the Theodosian Code," 137–39; Honoré, "Some Quaestors," 74; Matthews, *Laying Down the Law*, 171.

99  Honoré, "Making of the Theodosian Code," 159.

taken from these provincial copies rather than representing the original.[100] Another factor that impedes our ability to recover the original text of any given law is that the narrative framework that accompanied each individual law when it was first issued, which explained the circumstances that led to its creation, was intentionally omitted for the sake of brevity: "Furthermore, the very words themselves of the constitutions, in so far as they pertain to the essential matter, shall be preserved, but those words which were added not from the very necessity of sanctioning the law shall be omitted" (*CTh* 1.1.5).[101] We can get an idea of what these narratives would have looked like by reading the Tetrarchy's Edict of Maximum Prices, issued in 301 CE. The edict, which represents an attempt to address their troubled economy by setting the maximum prices that may be charged for goods and services, is prefaced by several paragraphs of introductory material. Here the emperors attribute the crisis to the greed of individuals. The edict's narrative framework does not yield concrete details about the situation on the ground in 301 CE, but it does afford us some insight as to how the Romans interpreted their economic crisis. The edict's preface demonstrates that they viewed the situation through the lens of individual morality.

There were other editorial practices for the Theodosian Code of which we should take note. The compilers of the Theodosian Code were given permission to alter the texts of the laws so as to make them clearer.[102] "In order that the law may be constrained by brevity and may be lucid with clarity, We grant to those men who are about to undertake this work the power to remove superfluous words, to add necessary words, to change ambiguities,

---

100 Matthews, *Laying Down the Law*, 163; see also 285–88 for a summary of the sources of the Code.

101 Justinian's *Codex* also refers to the suppression of "superfluous preambles" (Preface, section 2).

102 Honoré, "Making of the Theodosian Code," 165–66; Honoré, "Some Quaestors," 71.

and to emend incongruities. By these methods, of course, each constitution shall stand forth illuminated" (*CTh* 1.1.6). Honoré notes, however, that it was not a free-for-all and that when we can check their work (that is, when two or more versions of a given law exist), the compilers seem to have been more interested in polishing the language rather than altering its substance. Perhaps of more moment to us today was the requirement to use polished language, which was also a factor in the composition of the original laws. Cassiodorus (c. 485–c. 585 CE) makes it clear that the laws were to be composed in a certain style. A low style was employed for commoners, a mid-range style was employed for officials, and a high style was employed for the emperor.[103] What this meant in practice is that the *quaestor* who drafted the law had a vested interest in crafting an ornate, highly rhetorical piece of prose. His concern was not to be understood (!) but to impress. Officials who received new laws therefore had to "decode" them.[104] If contemporaries had to work to uncover the meaning of a recently passed law, it is no wonder that misinterpretations of older laws could occur. We can see evidence of such mistakes in the Theodosian Code.[105]

Multiple versions, missing opening narratives, later edits, all of these factors lead to the conclusion that the Theodosian Code is not a straightforward reflection of the circumstances that gave rise to the individual laws within it. We also cannot use the Code itself to determine the degree to which its laws were enforced once the Code was published. But we can say a fair amount about how this collection of laws was made and why it was made, and we can also see in this code a public, shared narrative, the story of how a just and good emperor relates to his grateful, obedient

---

103 Honoré, "Making of the Theodosian Code," 139–40.
104 Honoré, "Making of the Theodosian Code," 140–41.
105 For an example, see Matthews, *Laying Down the Law*, 254–70; on changing the wording of the original so that the meaning itself changes, see 261–63.

subjects. In some respects, the message of the Theodosian Code is the message of the imperial panegyrics. It too, presents to us an idealized portrait of imperial rule.

Moving on to the sixth century, Justinian's *Corpus Juris Civilis* refers to the three-part series of legal texts produced in his reign, the *Codex*, the *Institutes*, and the *Digest*.[106] The *Codex* and his *Novels* were the laws; the *Digest* consisted of the opinions and reasoning of jurists, and *Institutes* was a textbook for students of the law.[107] Justinian began work on his law code in 528 CE. As the preface to the *Codex* tells us, he set up a council to gather and revise imperial constitutions from Hadrian's time up to the present. The end result was to be general laws grouped according to subject matter and arranged in chronological order.[108] The first edition of the *Codex* was published in 529 CE, but this was quickly revised and a second edition was produced in 534 CE (as we also see from the preface to the *Codex*). This edition became the foundation for the codes of the Byzantine era.[109] The *Codex* adds some material not found in the Theodosian Code for the pre-Constantine period and some that came after the time of Theodosius, much of which was produced by Justinian himself.[110]

Justinian's legal texts show us an emperor who took the imperial ideology of the just and good lawmaker to a new level. Earlier we quoted his statement concerning the commission appointed to undertake the *Digest*, in which he declared, "it is from us that all their authority is derived" (*Dig. Const. Deo Auctore* 6, 530 CE). As Caroline Humfress has demonstrated, his novels show

---

106 For an overview of Byzantine law codes, see Stolte, "Justice," 691–98.
107 Matthews, *Laying Down the Law*, 11–12.
108 Discussed in Humfress, "Law and Legal Practice," 163.
109 Humfress, "Law and Legal Practice," 164.
110 Gillian Clark, *Women in Late Antiquity: Pagan and Christian Lifestyles* (Oxford: Oxford University Press, 1994), 8–9.

the emperor inserting himself into every practice and procedure, in both the administrative and ecclesiastical realms.[111] Justinian's conception of law was that it was shaped by God, but that he had the God-given right to issue it: "those to whom permission has been given by God to enact laws; We mean by this him who is invested with sovereignty" (Justinian, *Novel* 72 pr.); "The Emperor shall justly be regarded as the sole maker and interpreter of the laws" (Justinian, *Codex* 1.14.12).[112] We can see the links among his own legacy, God, and the law, in the first chapter of his *Novel* 47. This is addressed to John of Cappadocia who was the praetorian prefect.

> Wherefore We order that all those officials employed in drawing up documents or decisions, ... in this great city, or in other parts of the Empire, over which God has given Us the right to preside, shall begin as follows: 'The year of the reign of the Most Holy and August Emperor,' and, afterwards insert the name of the Consul for that year, and then the indiction, month, and day; in order that the date may be entirely preserved by the mention of the reigning sovereign and the order of the consulate, and the other formalities be observed, as is customary, and when this has been done no changes should be made ... documents shall be begun in the name of God, for instance: 'The eleventh year of the reign of the Most Holy Emperor Justinian, the second year after the Consulate of that most illustrious

---

111 Humfress, "Law and Legal Practice," 167–70. Both *Novel* 47 and *Novel* 24 below are discussed in Humfress, "Law and Legal Practice," 169–70, with regard to Justinian's extension of legal authority.

112 All translations of Justinian's novels and the *Codex* are taken from S.P. Scott, ed., *The Civil Law: Including the Twelve Tables, the Institutes of Gaius, the Rules of Ulpian, the Opinions of Paulus, the Enactments of Justinian, and the Constitutions of Leo* (Cincinnati: Central Trust Co., 1932; New York: AMS Press, 1973).

man, Flavius Belisarius, on the ... day of the Kalends of ...' Thus in all public documents, the year of the Empire, that of Our reign—so far as God may be pleased to prolong it—and, in the future, the names of succeeding Emperors, will be mentioned. This is perfectly clear, because at present the eleventh year of Our reign is written; but from the beginning of next April, the day upon which God invested Us with the government of the Empire, the twelfth year shall be stated; and so on, as long as God may permit Us to reign, so that this name may survive the laws, and the mention of the latter may remain immortal, while the commemoration of the Empire shall be introduced in all transactions for all time.

Justinian, although he often couched his policies in traditional language, had a radical program: his proposed changes in the areas of religion, the economy, administration, and foreign policy were intended to have totalizing and unifying effects. We can see this in his reform of the provincial governorship.

Bearing these things in mind, and recalling with honor the ancient institutions of the Republic, as well as the dignity of the Roman name, and being aware that ... in certain of Our provinces subject to both civil and military jurisdiction, the Governors were always quarrelling among themselves, and opposing one another, and, instead of accomplishing something beneficial to Our subjects, they, on the other hand, rather oppressed them, We have thought that it would be preferable to unite the civil and military jurisdictions into one, and again give the name of Praetor to the magistrate invested with this authority ... Being thus invested with great dignity, the Praetor would be terrible to robbers, and render it impossible for those guilty of injustice to escape. He could accomplish everything through his extraordinary power. (*Novel* 24, Chapter 1)

The language here at first suggests tradition (the Roman Republic), but Justinian quickly notes problems with the old way: the governors were discontented and there were quarrels leading to inefficiency. His revamping of this office is presented as a decided improvement, a wonderful boon to the power and prestige of the magistrates who will now be in a position to maintain order and security as never before. But this seeming increase in authority is immediately undercut, as Justinian continues, "but he shall maintain justice in every instance, and regulate his conduct by Our enactments, rendering judgment in accordance with them, so that Our subjects may also form their lives and their rules of conduct in conformity thereto; and he must, above all things, keep the fear of God and of Us in mind, and never plan anything in contravention of Our precepts."

Knowing the general trends and themes of the earlier imperial law codes illuminates Justinian's expansion of the centralizing power of the imperial office. And a similar type of analysis proves equally valuable for other codes of the Byzantine Empire. We compare below each code's proem with that of earlier precedents and see what stands out, what makes each at once part of a tradition and unique.

There were many new law codes produced in the Byzantine period after Justinian, but here we will consider only the most significant of the imperial codes.[113] In the eighth century CE, Leo the III published the *Ecloga* (from the Greek word, *eklogē*, "selection"). This was issued in 741 CE and was the first imperial law code to be issued in Greek in the Byzantine Empire. The code was issued in his own name and that of his son, his co-emperor,

---

113 Dates for the law codes discussed below follow the timeline of Zachary Chitwood, *Byzantine Legal Culture and the Roman Legal Tradition* (Cambridge, UK: Cambridge University Press, 2017), 867–1056.

Constantine V. This code was comprised of a selection from Justinian law and a revision of that law. The proem presents the code as a thank-offering to the Lord. The rule of revision set out there is worded a bit ambiguously. It has been interpreted as meaning either a "correction towards greater humanity" or simply a correction toward "greater clarity."[114] The intent was certainly to make the laws clearer and the emperor just as clearly had an interest in framing the law in thoroughly Christian terms. The entire proem is filled with references to the Christian God and to Scriptures. In its final section, the emperor writes that he hopes that in this work "the ancient jurisdiction of the Empire will be established in us for ever," which is followed by biblical quotations reiterating earlier statements about the Divine basis for law in human society.[115] This work, even more so than Justinian's, seeks to bring the Roman law of the past into the Christian present.[116]

The next major law code was published in the ninth century CE under Emperor Basil I. According to the *Life of Basil* 33:

> Upon finding that the secular laws contained much obscurity and confusion because of the juxtaposition of good as well as wicked laws, that is the indistinguishable and joint listing of valid and abrogated [laws], he fittingly corrected them according to what was suitable and what was possible, by removing the uselessness of the abrogated [laws] and cleansing the multitude of the valid [laws], and by placing the former infinity [of the laws] in chapters,

---

114 ἐπιδιόρθωσις εἰς τὸ φιλανθρωπότερον/*epidiorthosis eis to philanthropoteron*.
115 Translation by Freshfield, *Roman Law*, 42.
116 For its Christian character see, Humphreys, *Law, Power, and Imperial Ideology*, 81–129; Dieter Simon, "Legislation as Both a World Order and a Legal Order," in *Law and Society in Byzantium, Ninth-Twelfth Centuries*, eds. Angeliki E. Laiou and Dieter Simon (Washington, DC: Dumbarton Oaks Research Library and Collection, 1994), 12–16.

just as in a summary, so that they could be remembered easily.[117]

Basil produced two legal publications. The *Prochiron* contained Justinian law and some new laws. Its intent was to make clear which laws from the past were still valid. Old, abolished laws were put into one book for easy reference (*Prochiron* preface, ll. 77–82).[118] But there was also an apologetic intent. According to Chitwood: "From a political standpoint, the creation of the *Prochiron* was part of the Macedonian dynasty's reappropriation of *Romanitas*; by excerpting the laws of past pre-iconoclastic emperors, the creators of the *Prochiron* were in effect cementing the continuity of the Macedonian emperors with their pious predecessors."[119] After his reign, this work was expanded.

The *Eisagoge* also dates to this time.[120] Its proem was compiled by the patriarch Photius (patriarch 858–867; 877–886 CE). This law code also had a polemical thrust. The proem refers explicitly to the earlier code in these terms, the "nonsense promulgated by the Isaurians" (1.35).[121] The second and third titles spell out the separation of powers between the emperor and the patriarch over temporal and spiritual matters, respectively. This was likely a response to "the caesaropapist tendencies" exhibited in the proem of a previous code, the *Ecloga*, in which the emperor had likened himself to St. Peter; as Peter led the Apostles, so he, too, served as a shepherd to his flock.[122]

---

117 Translation by Chitwood, *Byzantine Legal Culture*, 25.
118 For the complicated nature of the *Prochiron* and its relationship to its predecessors, see Chitwood, *Byzantine Legal Culture*, 16–44.
119 Chitwood, *Byzantine Legal Culture*, 29.
120 *Eisagoge tou nomou* ("introduction to the law").
121 Trans. Aerts et al., "Prooimion of the Eisagoge," 97.
122 Chitwood, *Byzantine Legal Culture*, 31, citing Andreas Schminck, "Minima Byzantina," *Zeit-schrift der Savigny-Stiftung für Rechtsgeschichte: Romanistische Abteilung* 132.1 (2015): 474–78.

Leo VI, the successor of Basil I, published the *Basilika* ("royal laws"). This included those parts of the *Corpus Juris Civilis* that were still useful. Those parts that were "contradictory, obsolete, and redundant" were cut.[123] There were later interpolations to this code (which perhaps occurred after his reign). We can see how similar the concept of this code was to the *Prochiron*.

Later Byzantine emperors also felt the need to make pre-existing codes more "useful" and "clear," and several more versions of these earlier codes were produced. But throughout the Byzantine period, other types of legal material in addition to the imperial codes existed and were regularly used. These included commentaries, private collections, canon law, and syntheses of secular and ecclesiastical law on matters relating to the church (called *nomocanons*); laws for specific groups such as the *Farmer's Law*, the *Rhodian Sea Law*, the *Soldier's Law*, and the *Book of the Eparch* (which consists of laws pertaining to Byzantine guilds, professional and commercial ordinances).[124] The regulations for specific groups I mention only in passing, to show the range and types of laws that were prevalent in Byzantine society. These would of course be quite good sources for those interested in Byzantine economic history. But, as we are confining our study to broader categories of law, we now turn to ecclesiastical regulations.

### Ecclesiastical Law

As with the state, the church also had many different types of regulatory texts. Codes and novels included laws that pertained to the church and to correct religious belief. Such laws appear for instance at the end of the Theodosian Code or the beginning

---

123 J.H.A. Lokin, "The Significance of Law and Legislation in the Law Books of the Ninth to Eleventh Centuries," in *Law and Society in Byzantium, Ninth-Twelfth Centuries*, eds. Angeliki E. Laiou and Dieter Simon (Washington, DC: Dumbarton Oaks Research Library and Collection, 1994), 81, citing *Basilica-praefatio* lines 20–23.

124 The *nomocanon* first developed in the sixth century: Clark, *Women in Late Antiquity*, 12; Stolte, "Justice," 68.

of Justinian's *Codex*. Justinian's novels on the church were quite detailed, including, among other things, such matters as church financing and property, the charity work of bishops, the conduct of clergy and monks, the rights of the bishop's court, heresy, asylum, and the right of bishops to say which governors they wanted to have appointed over them (*Novel* 3; 5; 6; 7; 11; 14; 37; 79; 86; 131; 133).

Canon law is the church's own internal law. Such laws were intended to apply to the entire Christian community. They were at first created by ecumenical councils, dating from 325–787 CE. But beginning after the Council *in Trullo* (also known as the *Quinisextum* or *Penthekte*) the Byzantines added new rulings by the patriarchs in consultation with other spiritual leaders and also created authoritative commentary on the existing canons.[125] Canon law did not begin to be codified until 545 CE and before that time was no more consistent or standardized than secular law. Justinian in 545 CE decreed that the canons produced at Nicaea, Constantinople, Ephesus, and Chalcedon were law.

Internal rules of the Christian community were also collected into church manuals, also called handbooks or orders, into monastic rules, and into the foundation documents of monastic communities called *typika*. We will survey a few of the most significant church orders below. These Christian handbooks set out codes of conduct for the faithful. They also included some religious teachings. Beginning in the late first or second century CE, several were produced in various times and regions. In working with these texts, it is important to note that not every handbook was necessarily intended for the entire Christian community, but may rather reflect local practices and needs. It should not be taken for granted that they are an accurate reflection of how Christians actually conducted themselves without corroboration from other sources.

---

125 Stolte, "Justice," 68.

The *Didache* is the earliest church order. Several of the elements present in this early version are seen in later handbooks. Like later church orders, it purports to be teaching passed down to the church directly from the apostles. The text opens with a teaching about the "two ways," the way of life (godly living) and the way of death (ungodly living). It describes proper procedures for baptism, fasting, prayer, assemblies, and the celebration of the Eucharist. Different types of Christian leaders and their proper role in the community are outlined: teachers, apostles, prophets, bishops, and deacons. It closes with an exhortation to keep watch! and stay ready for the end times.

*The Apostolic Tradition* (also known as the *Apostolic Church Order* or *the Egyptian Church Order*; c. 300 CE) is a good example of why these church orders are difficult to use as historical documents. There is no complete manuscript of the text. It appears that it was originally composed in Greek, with translations into Latin, Ethiopic, Syriac, Arabic, Bohairic, and Sahidic Coptic. Material from it was incorporated into later church orders. The text is a living document, a set of practices, guidelines, and beliefs that was added to and transformed over time.[126] For example, the *Apostolic Tradition* contains a Eucharistic prayer that follows the ordination rite for a bishop. On this, Baldovin writes, "Clearly the document makes no pretense whatsoever that this is *the* eucharistic prayer of the Church. It is an example of a prayer given in a specific situation (the ordination of a bishop); later in the document ... it is clear that the prayers proposed are models and that the bishop gives thanks according to his ability .... There is a very real possibility that the *Apostolic Tradition* describes liturgies that never

---

126  On church orders as "living literature," see John F. Baldovin, "Hippolytus and the *Apostolic Tradition*: Recent Research and Commentary," *Theological Studies* 64 (2003): 534; 542; compare Paul F. Bradshaw, Maxwell E. Johnson and L. Edward Phillips, The Apostolic Tradition: *A Commentary*, ed. Harold W. Attridge (Minneapolis, MN: Fortress Press, 2002), 14.

## CHAPTER 3: PROHIBITION AND PRESCRIPTION

existed," that is, the prayers within the text are only to serve as models.[127]

Perhaps the handbook with the greatest geographical spread was the *Apostolic Constitutions*. This text dates to the end of the fourth CE and its provenance is unknown. It incorporates earlier material from several pre-existing church orders and when compared to other manuals is seen to be particularly full, comprising eight books. It is framed as a set of directives originating from the apostles and includes general biblical precepts; the appointment of bishops, presbyters, deacons, readers, widows, etc.; church mechanics; and organization.

Comparing and contrasting the orders is a useful method of approach for this genre. If we compare the role of the deaconess in this text to the description of this position in other manuals, we can see that the *Apostolic Constitutions* has more sections on the deaconess. (The deaconess is discussed in sections 2.26; 2.57–2.58; 3.7; 3.11; 3.15; 3.16; 8.13; 8.19–20; 8.28; 8.31). It includes some information not found in other church orders, such as how she is to be ordained by the bishop, the fact that she is entitled to take oblation before virgins and widows, and the fact that she is entitled to one part of any leftover oblation. But it also repeats several items found in the Ethiopic version of the *Didaskalia* (a church order originally composed in Greek and dating to the first half of the third century CE), such as the fact that she is to be subordinate to the deacon, to mediate between other women and the deacon and other women and the bishop, to act as a doorkeeper at assemblies directing the women where to sit, and to assist women in baptism with their clothes, for modesty's sake (so that they are not viewed by men in a state of undress).[128]

---

127 Baldovin, "Hippolytus and the *Apostolic Tradition*," 538, 542; Baldovin contains an overview of the current scholarly theories on this work.

128 The deaconess is discussed in 2.26; 2.57–2.58; 3.16; 6.17 of *The Ethiopic Didascalia*.

The *Apostolic Constitutions* pays more attention than other church manuals to the position of the deaconess with respect to other minor clergy and other female groups (such as widows and virgins). The Syriac *Didaskalia* states only that she is to be honored next after the deacons (9).[129] Like the Syriac *Didaskalia*, however, the deaconess is to minister to the needy and visit the sick (Syriac *Didaskalia* 16). It is a little different, however, in the specification of her service duties. In the *Apostolic Constitutions*, the deaconess is "to carry messages, to travel about, to minister, and to serve" (3.19).

On the evidence of the church orders then, the role of the deaconess was not set in stone. In the Syriac *Didaskalia*, the deaconess is empowered to provide some religious teaching after baptism, a duty not included in other church manuals:

> And when she who is being baptized has come up from the water, let the deaconess receive her, and teach and instruct her how the seal of baptism ought to be (kept) unbroken in purity and holiness. For this cause we say that the ministry of a woman deacon is especially needful and important. For our Lord and Saviour also was ministered unto by women ministers, Mary Magdalene, and Mary the daughter of James and mother of Jose, and the mother of the sons of Zebedee, with other women beside.[130]

This must be considered an exception to the rule that women should not teach that appears in 3.6 and that, curiously enough, is justified on the same basis, that is, with reference to the fact that there were female disciples working alongside the apostles—but they had not been commanded, as the male disciples

---

129 The only complete copy of the *Didaskalia*.
130 Translated by R. Hugh Connolly, *Didascalia Apostolorum* (Oxford: Clarendon Press, 1929), 61.

had, to teach. The church orders also indicate that there was disagreement over the role of the deaconess with respect to the Eucharist. Should a deaconess administer it or not? In 1.24–28, the Bohairic version of the *Apostolic Tradition* (which is a nineteenth century translation, based on the Sahidic Coptic version), the apostles discuss whether or not to appoint deaconesses and use biblical grounds for arguing that they should not administer the Eucharist. This passage on the duties of the deaconess is framed almost like a truncated rabbinic discussion among the apostles: "Cephas said, 'Some say it becomes the women to pray standing'" (1.27).[131] In the *Testament of our Lord* 2.20, a church order that dates to approximately the fifth century CE, the deaconess carries the Eucharist to women who were too sick to attend church services.

These orders, as noted above, do not appear to have been universally dispersed or regarded as universally valid for all Christian communities. Their distribution pattern indicates that they were nevertheless used by more than one community. The rules in these church manuals were directed toward both religious leaders and laypersons. In the type of internal rules that we cover next, the regulations were intended only for monastics and, for the most part, only for specific monastic communities. Having made this generalization, however, there is some evidence that a few Late Antique monastic rules may have been adopted by more than one community, such as that of Pachomius, who lived in the mid-fourth century CE in Egypt, or Basil of Caesarea, Archbishop of Caesarea (370–379 CE), who had an interest in monastic reforms and produced both Longer Rules and Shorter Rules. Several Syrian Rules were also produced in Late Antiquity. The rules in all of these covered such aspects of monastic life as dietary and behavioral prohibitions, prayer times, and work details.

---

131 Translated by Henry Tattam, *The Apostolical Constitutions; or, Canons of the Apostles, in Coptic* (London: Printed for the Oriental translation fund of Great Britain and Ireland, 1848), 28.

Beyond their obvious usage as a window into the day-to-day life of monastic communities, we can use this source type in comparison with other evidence to obtain a fuller picture of religious life and interactions between orders and the surrounding society. As an example, we briefly take up Shenoute's *Canons*. Shenoute (347–465 CE) was an Egyptian saint and the third head of the White Monastery Foundation, monastic communities in Upper Egypt. From his extant writings, Bentley Layton has collected several hundred rules organized in nine books and to these rules, we apply two types of approach or method of analysis.[132]

Scattered throughout the rules are numerous references to the regulation of food and drink. From the number of these, we can infer that this was a matter of particular concern to the community.[133] And from the number of condemnatory references to food snatchers, that is, to stealthy eaters, we can further deduce that monks struggled to conform to the dietary demands of the ascetic lifestyle. In this instance, the straightforward reading already reveals this information, although in fact we may learn even more about Shenoute's attitude toward food and the role of food in this monastic community and in Late Antiquity Christianity more generally, if we were to compare and contrast other writings of or about Shenoute with the *Canons*.[134]

Let us take then this second type of approach in regard to a specific rule, *Canons* 9.479. This is a case in which a comparison with other sources helps us better understand the rule. In 9.479,

---

[132] Bentley Layton, *The Canons of Our Fathers: Monastic Rules of Shenoute* (Oxford: Oxford University Press, 2014), 3–5. The numbering in this section is based on Layton's translation.

[133] Layton analyzes the function of the food rules in the *Canons* in Bentley Layton, "Social Structure and Food Consumption in an Early Christian Monastery: The Evidence of Shenoute's *Canons* and the White Monastery Federation," *Le Muséon* 115 (2002): 25–55.

[134] See, for example, Diana Robinson, *Food, Virtue, and the Shaping of Early Christianity* (Cambridge, UK: Cambridge University Press, 2020), especially 152–56.

## CHAPTER 3: PROHIBITION AND PRESCRIPTION

Shenoute advises the monastic community not to use violence against pagans and not to threaten to take them to the magistrates—unless he himself has sent them to do so. From this, we infer that Shenoute wanted to retain the right to use violence if he felt the situation called for it. The evidence of his *Life* and his discourses reveal that Shenoute had been in situations where he felt violence was the appropriate response. He describes on several occasions how he acted with violence against the property and the person of Gesios. Gesios was the Coptic name of Flavius Aelius Gessius, governor of the Roman province of the Thebaid (376–380 CE), a local rich man with whom Shenoute had an acrimonious relationship.[135] "And also when I gave him a thump on the chest and said to him, 'Until they cut out your tongue, with which you uttered blasphemy, doubting that Jesus was God!'" (*Let our Eyes*).[136] The discourses of Shenoute indicate that such instances of violence did not pass without comment and that Shenoute had had to respond to accusations arising from his conflict with Gesios and from his attack on a pagan temple (*Sermon* A26), and that he had created enemies for himself by such actions (such as Count Chrysippus, who

---

135 For the identity of Gesios and the conflict between Shenoute and Gesios, see David Brakke and Andrew Crislip, *Selected Discourses of Shenoute the Great: Community, Theology, and Social Conflict in Late Antique Egypt*, translated with introductions (Cambridge, UK: Cambridge University Press, 2015), 193; 199–200.

136 Shenoute, *Let Our Eyes* is a discourse found in a collection of his miscellaneous works, *Varia,* translated by Stephen Emmel in *Select Discourses,* 209. Shenoute raids Gesios's house, stealing the idols from it and destroying them: *Life* 125–27; *Sermon* A26; *Discourses* 4, *Work* 5; *Discourses* 8, *Work* 20; Shenoute burns a pagan temple: *Sermon* A26 (pp. 238–39 in *Selected Discourses*); *Let our Eyes*, in *Varia* (p. 211 in *Selected Discourses*). In the *Life of Shenoute* 128–30, at a synod to condemn the heretic Nestorius, Shenoute strikes Nestorius, who was present, in the chest and admonishes him. Although the episode is thought to be fictitious, there being no record of Cyril and Nestorius meeting at the council of Ephesus—see David N. Bell, *The Life of Shenoute by Besa: Introduction, Translation, and Notes* (Kalamazoo, MI: Cistercian Publications, 1983), 33, n. 99—it does show that violence against the enemies of God was considered to be justified in Shenoute's eyes.

stood by Gesios, in *Discourses* 8, *Work* 20). On the basis of this comparison of sources then, we might conclude that Shenoute's experiences had taught him that one should carefully consider whether it was worth the trouble and ill will that the use of violence might incur.

The Pachomian and Basilian traditions were to some degree each influential in later Byzantine monasticism, but generally speaking, the Byzantines did not follow any overarching rule, whether one from the past or a new, contemporary rule. Rather, each monastery or set of monasteries had its own rules and these are found in foundation documents called *typika* (in the plural; *typicon* in the singular). Such documents included a narrative concerning the founding of the monastery and laid out its property, its rights, and its obligation to commemorate its founders and benefactors. *Typika* included also the rules of conduct that would govern day-to-day life, such as work requirements, respect for superiors, relationship to outsiders, and dietary regimens. Later there developed *typika* that only describe the liturgies, setting out the entire liturgical year in great detail.[137] There are great variations among the extant *typika* and they were not necessarily created at the time of the community's founding. Like monastic rules, the *typika* were sometimes added to over time.[138] They provided a legal basis and protection for the community so they were very important documents, hence the injunctions to read them aloud at regular intervals, which is mentioned in several *typika*.[139]

---

137 Giles Constable, "Preface," in *Byzantine Monastic Foundation Documents: A Complete Translations of the Surviving Founders' Typika and Testaments. Volume 1*, eds. John Thomas and Angela Constantinides, with the assistance of Giles Constable (Washington, DC: Dumbarton Oaks Research Library and Collection, 2000), xxiii; John Thomas and Angela Constantinides, *BMFD* 1:193. In what follows, references to the work of Thomas and Constantinides will be abbreviated as *BMFD*.

138 As for example in the case of the *Precepts of Pachomius* or the *typika* of Evergetis, Kosmosoteira, and Phoberos (*BMFD* 1:34).

139 Constable, "Preface," xi–xiii.

## CHAPTER 3: PROHIBITION AND PRESCRIPTION

The usefulness of the monastic foundation documents varies a good deal. In some cases, it is difficult to find corroborating evidence against which to test any statements about the monastery's history or its relationship to the outside world. But there are occasionally meaty exceptions. The foundation documents for the Lavra Monastery are a good example.[140] This monastery, located on Mount Athos in northern Greece, was founded by Athanasios the Athonite. There are several foundation documents for it. Three of these were composed by the founder of the community, Athanasios, and two are imperial documents. In this case then, we can compare and contrast the founder's perspective on the community across time and also compare and contrast his views with those of other people to gain a fuller perspective. It is also a particularly good set of documents for the study of genre, as not all of them are typical *typika*, with one document being in testament form; there is also evidence of borrowing from earlier Byzantine testaments and *typika*.

We can trace in the documents a debate over the appropriate level and type of economic activities for the brothers. Athanasios's rule of 963 CE refers to metal works, muleteers, shipwrights, carpenters, and workers in the vineyards (30). That this was a source of dispute is made clear from the *Typikon* of Emperor John Tzimiskes (dating to 971–972 CE; 13; 15) and from the fact that in his second rule (dating to 973–975 CE), Athanasios denies that he now champions commercial activity and defends the steps he had taken in the past to cultivate fields and vineyards, characterizing it as a necessity due to the isolated, inaccessible nature of the community's location (9–11).

When considering how to approach legal materials for historical use, we must keep in mind the relationship between the texts—with their conventional formats and language—and reality: how did people interact with or use these legal materials

---

140  *BMFD* 1:193–293, with translations of the five documents by George Dennis and Timothy Miller.

## SOURCES IN LATE ANTIQUITY AND BYZANTIUM

in their day-to-day lives? We end this chapter therefore with a discussion of how all of these competing legal systems might have looked on the ground. Given the span of papyrological evidence, we have more information about actual court cases for Late Antiquity than for Byzantium, so the following applies to the earlier period.

When it came to the settlement of disputes between parties in Late Antiquity, there was more than just written law to consider.[141] A dispute could be settled by arbitration, mediation, or negotiation.[142] In arbitration, a third party was selected to serve as arbiter and the parties agreed to accept his decision, which was enforced by the praetor. An arbiter could not be forced to serve, but if he agreed to take on the job, he had to complete it (*CTh* 2.9; *Digest* 4.8.3.1).[143] Mediation was a private, informal adjudication by a third party; negotiation was an attempt by the parties concerned to come to a mutually beneficial decision.[144]

If an individual decided to go to secular court, fees would have to be paid. A fourth-century CE inscription from North Africa provides some specifics:

> The payment which must be made to the head of the governor's staff for appointing an official [to serve a summons on a defendant]: within the town, five modii (bushels) of wheat or the price thereof; within one mile of the town, seven modii of wheat or the price thereof; for every additional ten miles, two modii of wheat or the price thereof; if the official is

---

141 Jill Harries, "Resolving Disputes: The Frontiers of Law in Late Antiquity," in *Law, Society and Authority in Late Antiquity*, ed. Ralph W. Mathisen (Oxford: Oxford University Press, 2001), 68–82.

142 Harries, *Law and Empire*, 172; for details of the options available to people for private disputes in the age of Justinian, see Humfress, "Law and Legal Practice," 175–84.

143 Harries, *Law and Empire*, 177.

144 Harries, *Law and Empire*, 187–88.

## CHAPTER 3: PROHIBITION AND PRESCRIPTION

required to travel overseas, then one hundred modii of wheat or the price thereof is required.[145]

But secular courts were not the only option. In their own communities, bishops acted to resolve disputes, although this was not a requirement; that is, a lay Christian could go to secular court if he wished, although it was discouraged in internal Christian law (*Apostolic Constitutions* 6.46; for clergy: Council of Chalcedon, *Canon* 9). Laws regulating the reach of the ecclesiastical courts changed over time. For example, in 333 CE, Constantine made it law that a case could "be brought before the bishop even over one side's objection," but as later laws do not confirm this, we must assume that this law was later revoked (*Sirmonian Constitution* 1).[146] Some laws apparently sought to confine the jurisdiction of bishops to matters pertaining to religion (*CTh* 16.11.1 and 16.2.23; Valentinian, *Novel* 35). Other laws stated that non-Christians could choose to appear before a bishop's court (*CTh* 1.27.1; *CJ* 1.4.8). According to Justinian's *Novel* 86, a private person could appeal to a bishop's court if he did not like the ruling he obtained from a governor. Secular officials were to enforce the decision of bishops (*CTh* 1.27.2; *Sirmonian Constitution* 1).

The Syrian *Didaskalia* offers the most detail on the bishop's court. *Didaskalia* 4–12 lays out the duties of a bishop and his relationship to the congregation, with particular stress on the character of the bishop and his responsibility to judge and rebuke with mercy.[147]

---

145 Translation taken from Kelly, *Ruling*, 108, citing Andre Chastagnol, *L'Album municipal de Timgad* (Bonn: Rudolf Habelt, 1978), 75–76, quoting lines 12–22.

146 Georg Schmelz, "Clerics as Arbiters in Christian Egypt," in *Law and Legal Practice in Egypt from Alexander to the Arab Conquest*, eds. James G. Keenan, J.G. Manning, and Uri Yiftach-Firanko (Cambridge: Cambridge University Press, 2014), 522.

147 Discussed in Schmelz, "Clerics as Arbiters in Christian Egypt," 520.

As Noel E. Lenski has demonstrated, the lines between the secular courts' jurisdiction and the ecclesiastical courts' jurisdiction were blurred; bishops seemed to have authority to impose punishments just as secular officials could.[148] Harries argues that overall, the bulk of the evidence points to the fact that bishops acted as arbiters and mediators.[149] Schmelz and Kotsifou demonstrate from the evidence of papyri from Egypt that not only bishops, but also other types of clerics and monks, were appealed to by the populace, by Christians and non-Christians alike, to act as arbiters and mediators.[150] Taken as a whole, the evidence suggests that the system was rather flexible, with some overlapping jurisdictions between secular and ecclesiastical courts and options for negotiation at many stages of the process.

The legal system of Late Antiquity was not rigid; there was a fluidity to it characteristic of ancient societies. But the above survey of so many types of imperial laws and regulations has also highlighted the fact that laws would have regulated many aspects of life for the average person. The Byzantine refrain: the law is obscure, let us make it clear! might lead us to conclude that society was practically negligent in its disregard for having one clear, universal set of laws. But what a concern for law and order looks like in that period of history is just what we see in our Late Antique and Byzantine sources: multiple, repeated attempts to clarify and update imperial law on the one hand, and

---

148 Noel E. Lenski, "Evidence for the *Audienta episcopalis* in the New Letters of Augustine," in *Law, Society and Authority in Late Antiquity*, ed. Ralph W. Mathisen (Oxford: Oxford University Press, 2001), 83–97; see also Schmelz, "Clerics as Arbiters in Christian Egypt," 517–29 and Chrysi Kotsifu, "Monks as Mediators in Christian Egypt," in *Law and Legal Practice in Egypt from Alexander to the Arab Conquest*, eds. James G. Keenan, J.G. Manning, and Uri Yiftach-Firanko (Cambridge: Cambridge University Press, 2014), 530–40.

149 Harries, "Resolving Disputes," 69–82; see also Harries, *Law and Empire*, 191 to 211.

150 Schmelz, "Clerics as Arbiters in Christian Egypt," 517–29; Kotsifou, "Monks as Mediators," 530–40.

on the other, the production of numerous regulations governing specific groups or limited spheres of activity (such as church life or guilds). The fact that they kept making improvements tells us that the rule of law and proper conduct were important to them. The amount of effort put into creating codes of conduct for the political, social, and religious realms is a noteworthy characteristic of Late Antique and Byzantine societies.

CHAPTER 4

# Literary Letter Collections: The Rhetorical and the Pragmatic

This chapter deals with literary letter collections. Literary letters refer to compositions that have been preserved in manuscripts. They were written with an eye to proper literary form and were intended to impress. These differ from individual letters as they were brought together for a particular purpose, selected and arranged to produce a certain effect. Letter collections became popular in the fourth century CE and enjoyed continued popularity in the Byzantine period. As demonstrated below, such letters, although they may have an intimate feel, were not intended to be private. They do not always make good sources for contemporary events, as at some periods the fashion was to close out the world and write in a vacuum. Even those that appear to provide firsthand observations may have hidden agendas. In what follows, we discuss the norms that shaped the composition of letter collections in Late Antiquity and Byzantium, from structure to selection of content. As we will see, these sources give information about several aspects of Late Antique and Byzantine society, including the social and intellectual life of elites, bishops and their congregations, emperors and religious officials, and emperors and subjects, along with their doctrinal disputes.

To begin with, how were letter collections created? Not every letter collection that we have was necessarily intended by the author. Any friend, disciple, or admirer could make up a collection of an individual's letters without permission.[151] Bishop Paulinus of Nola (c. 352/353–431 CE), for example, did not collect his letters and the manuscript tradition is not consistent,

---

151 A.R. Littlewood, "An 'Ikon of the Soul': The Byzantine Letter," *Visible Language* 10.3 (1976): 204.

which suggests that there was in fact no one archetype (*Letter* 41.1).¹⁵²

In some cases, the author intended to publish the letters even as he was composing them. Symmachus, a prominent fourth-century Roman statesman and orator, was one of first to consciously attempt to make his letter collection into a sort of autobiography; it was to be his public legacy.¹⁵³ In the first letter of his collection, Sidonius Apollinaris (c. 430–489 CE), describes how he went about creating it and makes reference in the process to Symmachus's collection, which had already become famous:

> With all the influence you derive from a genius for sound advice, you have long urged me to correct, revise, and bring together in one volume the more finished of those occasional letters which matters, men, and times have drawn from me: I am to set presumptuous foot where Symmachus of the ample manner, and Pliny of the perfected art have gone before .... If the tooth of jealousy spares these extravagances of mine, volume shall follow upon volume, all full-brimming with my most copious flow of correspondence. Farewell (*Letter* 1.1–4, written c. 477 CE to his friend Constantius).¹⁵⁴

Symmachus here is classified with other great letter writers from

---

152 Discussed in Catherine Conybeare, *Paulinus Noster: Self and Symbols in the Letters of Paulinus of Nola* (Oxford: Oxford University Press, 2000), 15; for a fuller discussion of the motives behind collections of bishops' letters, see Pauline Allen, "Rationales for Episcopal Letter-Collections in Late Antiquity," in *Collecting Early Christian Letters: From the Apostle Paul to Late Antiquity*, eds. Bronwen Neil and Pauline Allen (Cambridge: Cambridge University Press, 2015), 18–34.

153 Michele Renee Salzman, "Introduction," in *The Letters of Symmachus: Book 1*, trans. Michele Renee Salzman and Michael Roberts, with general introduction and commentary by Michele Renee Salzman (Atlanta: Society of Biblical Literature, 2011), xiv.

154 Translated by O.M. Dalton, *The Letters of Sidonius*, vol. 1 (Oxford: Clarendon Press, 1915), 1–2.

Roman history, such as Pliny the Younger (and Cicero in 1.2). Michele Salzman has demonstrated that Symmachus and his son collected Books 1–7 of his letters with the intention to publish. But Books 8–10 appear to be a later addition, added by an unidentified party. His letters were considered to be of general interest because the addressees were important figures of the day; they were also considered to be models of style.[155]

Not only could letters be added to a given collection at a later date, but there could also be later editing to individual letters within a collection, either by the author himself or by someone else. For example, the first letter in the collection of St. Symeon the New Theologian shows signs of editing. This could have been done by Symeon himself or by Nicetas, his disciple.[156] In this case, the design of the editor is clear: the wording needed to be changed because it included criticisms of the established hierarchy. "An attempt to forestall opposition was made by someone who was concerned that it should be accepted, and therefore wished it to be circulated as the work of an author of unimpeachable orthodoxy."[157]

In short, there are a range of factors that may have fed into any given letter collection, and we are not always able to say how a collection came into being. For Byzantine collections in particular, we rarely know either the origins of the collection or its original arrangement.[158]

---

155 Michele Renee Salzman, "Travel and Communication in *The Letters of Symmachus*," in *Travel, Communication and Geography in Late Antiquity: Sacred and Profane*, eds. Linda Ellis and Frank L. Kidner (Aldershot, UK/Burlington, VT: Ashgate Publishing, 2004; New York: Routledge, 2016), 82. Citations refer to the Routledge edition. For a fuller discussion see Salzman, "Introduction," liv–lxi.

156 H.J.M. Turner, ed. and trans., *The Epistles of St Symeon the New Theologian*, edited with an introduction, translation, and notes (Oxford: Oxford University Press, 2009), 15.

157 Turner, *Epistles*, 16.

158 Margaret Mullet, *Theophylact of Ochrid: Reading the Letters of a Byzan-

Letter collections from Late Antiquity to Byzantium share some common features. Literary letters needed to be polished works, with proper attention to style and vocabulary.[159] As we discuss below, a number of handbooks existed to help orient letter writers to the proper style. It was also commonplace to praise the style of the recipient and to denigrate one's own style. Sidonius Apolloniarius, for example, introduced briefly above, begins his letter collection with an expression of nervousness at his presumption in attempting to emulate the great letter writers of the past. "I have always been horribly conscious how far I fall short of these great examples" (*Letter* 1.2).[160]

Literary letters, whether intended by the author for publication or not, were not understood to be strictly private.[161] Symmachus's letters were read aloud and shared.[162] While at the palace for a public performance of poetry, Libanius took the opportunity to share a letter he had just received. "After reading your letter and admiring it, I got in ahead of the poet and used the gathering to read out the letter, and there was no one who could stand to listen in silence!" (*Letter* B107).[163] In a letter to the bishop of Kerkyra, Theophylact of Ochrid wrote, "For it is the function of the letter to chatter, not to be discreet" (G75, II, 401.35–36).[164]

---

tine *Archbishop* (Aldershot, UK: Variorum, 1997), 19.

159 For the Byzantine period, see Margaret Mullett, "The Classical Tradition in the Byzantine Letter," in *Byzantium and the Classical Tradition*, eds. Margaret Mullet and Roger Scott (Birmingham: Centre for Byzantine Studies, 1981; repr., *Letters, Literacy and Literature in Byzantium*, Aldershot, UK/Burlington, VT: Ashgate, 2007), 78–79; Littlewood, "'Ikon of the Soul,'" 201; 203–04.

160 For the Byzantine period, see Littlewood, "'Ikon of the Soul,'" 201.

161 Conybeare, *Paulinus Noster*, 41–50.

162 Salzman, "Travel and Communication," 81; Salzman, "Introduction," liii.

163 Trans. Bradbury, *Selected Letters*, 147.

164 Translated by Mullet, *Theophylact of Ochrid*, 18; for a fuller discussion of letters as public performance in Byzantine period, see 39–40. The "G" designation in the numbering of the letters refers to the numbering

Beyond any possible public audience, the contents of the letter would typically be known to the letter carrier. The letter carrier had an important role to play in the process of communication by letter. He, like the letter itself, operated as a stand-in for the presence of the sender and provided additional information to the recipient.[165] In a letter to Paulinus of Nola and his wife Therasia, Augustine the Bishop of Hippo describes the letter carriers Romanus and Agilis as being "like another letter of yours, a letter that hears my words and replies and is like the sweetest part of your presence" (*Letter* 31.2).[166] Symmachus mentions the role of the letter carrier often, depicting him as someone who would provide further oral information of a private nature, as for example in *Letter* 1.11.2, when he presses the letter carrier for more news of his father-in-law's travel plans.[167] In a letter of Libanius written in the summer 362 CE to Anatolius, Libanius writes: "I'd recount it to you if you didn't have with you the worthy Olympius, who'll speak better than a letter can and who has wept with me, extended his hand to me and knows everything" (*Letter* 43.2).[168] In a letter from Athanasius I (patriarch of Constantinople 1289–1293 and 1303–1309 CE) to an official, he writes, "To prevent the man who brings my message from saying one thing instead of another, I have made use of a letter with which to inform you" (*Letter* 8).[169] The letter carrier might

---

in Gautier's two volume edition, Paul Gautier, *Theophylacte d'Achrida: Introduction, Texte, Traduction et Notes* (Thessalonique: Association de Recherches Byzantines, 1980–1986).

165  Conybeare, *Paulinus Noster*, 39.

166  For full discussion of the role of the letter carrier with special attention to the Christian community, see Conybeare, *Paulinus Noster*, 31–40.

167  Salzman, "Introduction," liii, n. 197.

168  Trans. Bradbury, *Selected Letters*, 72.

169  Translated by Alice-Mary Talbot, *The Correspondence of Athanasius I, Patriarch of Constantinople: Letters to the Emperor Andronicus II, Members of the Imperial Family, and Officials*, an edition, translation, and commentary by Alice-Mary Maffry Talbot (Washington, DC: Dumbarton Oaks Center for Byzantine Studies, 1975), 23.

also be in charge of delivering the gifts that often accompanied a letter.[170]

Two main handbooks have come down to us on literary letters and we can often see the guidelines from these handbooks reflected in extant literary letters from Late Antiquity and Byzantium. One is a handbook incorrectly attributed to Demetrius of Phalerum, titled *Typoi Epistolikoi* or *Epistolary Types*. The dating is not precise, but it is believed that this work had its origins in the Hellenistic period, around 200 BCE, but was added to and revised over time, up until about 300 CE. This work consists of a description of twenty-one letter types, with examples of each. It was intended as a style guide, providing an overview of the main components for each type and a brief model.[171] The types are listed in the preface and include the "friendly, commendatory, blaming, reproachful, consoling, censorious, admonishing, threatening, vituperative, praising, advisory, supplicatory, inquiring, responding, allegorical, accounting, accusing, apologetic, congratulatory, ironic, thankful."[172]

The second work is the *Epistolimaioi Characteres* or *Epistolary Styles*. There are two manuscript traditions, one attributed to Libanius and one attributed to Proclus the Neo-Pythagorean, and the two have differences in the "title, text, and the arrangement of contents."[173] The actual author is unknown, and the text is dated anywhere from the fourth to the sixth century CE. The opening proposes to lay out every type of letter, explaining what is customary to say in each, in order that people may write them with great precision and skill (1). There are forty-one types in this handbook, overlapping with the earlier manual and adding

---

170 Conybeare, *Paulinus Noster*, 26–31 discusses gifts accompanying letters; for the Byzantine period, see Mullet, "Classical Tradition," 89.
171 Abraham J. Malherbe, *Ancient Epistolary Theorists* (Atlanta, GA: Scholars Press, 1988), 4.
172 Translation by Malherbe, *Ancient Epistolary Theorists*, 31.
173 Malherbe, *Ancient Epistolary Theorists*, 5.

## CHAPTER 4: LITERARY LETTER COLLECTIONS

others, such as the "erotic" or the "enigmatic."[174] Malherbe suggests that these handbooks were probably not used by the common man but were rather consulted by professional letter writers.[175] At the very least, it was educated elites who had leisure to consult handbooks of style and to whom a reputation for proper style would matter. Letters also served an important social function for elites to which we now turn.

Salzman has demonstrated the role of letters in networking among elites in Late Antiquity. Using the letters of Symmachus as an example, we can see how he used this medium to stay in touch with other members of the elite, to maintain close and useful connections, and also to enhance his personal reputation as a man of culture and education. His letters reveal that Symmachus wanted to be associated with the traditional values of Roman elites.[176] Hence, "Symmachus' limited list of travel destinations and descriptions casts him in the image of the traditional Roman senator and land owner, enjoying the pleasures of a private life surrounded by powerful friends and family."[177] In *Letter* 1.11 for example, in which he corresponds with the elder Symmachus about an upcoming family party to be held on a family estate in celebration of his wife's birthday, Symmachus writes, "I give you my word that the gentlemen's table here shall lack for nothing" (*Letter* 1.11.2).[178]

Through the letters Symmachus was able to exercise his influence by participating in a constant exchange of favors. The collection is full of letters of requests for favors on behalf of himself or of friends and acquaintances, with letters of recommendation

---

174  Trans. Malherbe, *Ancient Epistolary Theorists*, 67.
175  Malherbe, *Ancient Epistolary Theorists*, 7; Malherbe's introduction provides a full treatment of the history of the genre and other writings from antiquity about letter writing.
176  Salzman, "Introduction," xliv–xlv.
177  Salzman, "Travel and Communication," 88.
178  Translation by Salzman, *Letters of Symmachus*, 32.

being very prominent.[179] This is also the case in the letters of the Gallo-Roman aristocrat, Sidonius Apollonarius, who became the Bishop of Auvergne (Clermont).

> The Intendant of Supplies has personally presented the letter in which you commend him as your old friend to my new judgement. I am greatly indebted to him, but most of all to yourself for this evidence of your resolve to assume my friendship certain and proof against all suspicion. I welcome, I eagerly embrace this opportunity of acquaintance, and of intimacy, since my desire to oblige you cannot but draw closer the bonds which already unite us. But please commend me in my turn to his vigilant care, commend, that is, my cause and my repute. For I rather fear that there may be an uproar in the theatres if the supplies of grain run short, and that the hunger of all the Romans will be laid to my account. I am on the point of dispatching him immediately to the harbour in person, because news is to hand that five ships from Brindisi have put in at Ostia laden with wheat and honey. A stroke of energy on his part, and we should have these cargoes ready in no time for the expectant crowds; he would win my favour, I the people's, and he and I together yours. Farewell. (Sidonius Apollonarius, *Letter* 1.10.1-2, to his friend Campanianus, 468 CE)[180]

The theme of friendship evident in the letter is a regular epistolary theme. In a letter from Symmachus to Ausonius, Symmachus reproaches Ausonius for his long silence and stresses how important their friendship is to him: "I am determined to maintain frequent communication with you .... For I have nowhere

---

179  Salzman, "Introduction," xlv.
180  Trans. Dalton, *Letters of Sidonius*, 25–26.

invested the effort of friendship as well" (*Letter* 1.34).¹⁸¹ This reference to the investment put into friendship is perhaps an allusion to the networking function discussed above: maintaining friendships took work, but the payoffs were potentially huge.¹⁸² We can see the role that letters play in connecting elites with social and political honor in the following quote from a letter of Libanius to Spectatus, dated to 356/357 CE:

> [T]he civic duty to which our cousin has been summoned ought to be confirmed by a 'nod' from the emperor, while a letter needs to go to Sabinus conferring a higher rank, so that he is not left behind by those to whom he is superior in learning. That way he won't seem to be employing friends weaker than other people. Neither is it tolerable for me nor noble for you that his case offer any grounds for criticism of you and me. (*Letter* 2.2–3)¹⁸³

Letters of recommendation abound not only in the collection of Symmachus, but in many others, such as those of Libanius quoted above, Synesius of Cyrene, or, to give a Byzantine example, Michael Psellos.¹⁸⁴ Christian bishops, like Sidonius Apollinaris, Basil, and Augustine, often used the medium of the letter to act

---

181  Trans. Salzman, *Letters of Symmachus*, 70.

182  Salzman, *Letters of Symmachus*, 78 notes that Symmachus's friendship with Ausonius was "highly advantageous."

183  Trans. Bradbury, *Selected Letters*, in *Selected Letters*, 28–29; for friendship in Byzantine letters, see Littlewood, 222.

184  The letters of Synesius of Cyrene (second half of the fourth century) contain several letters of recommendation. In *Letter* 102, a letter for friendship and protection for one Sosenas whose good education is going to waste, Synesius asks Pylaemenes to introduce Sosenas to any friends of his that Sosenas may need when he comes to the imperial city to seek his fortune. On Michael Psellos, see Michael Jeffreys and Marc D. Lauxtermann, eds., *The Letters of Psellos: Cultural Networks and Historical Realities* (Oxford: Oxford University Press, 2017); see also from the ninth century, Ignatios the Deacon, *Letter* 49, in which a favor is asked for a friend, a monk in search of a bishopric.

as patrons, to assist the oppressed, or to fulfill their function as mediators. There are numerous examples from which we might choose. Augustine, for instance, in *Letter* 247, seeks tax relief for tenant farmers.[185] Basil of Caesarea acts as a mediator in a letter to one Harmatius, in which he asks this pagan father not to be angry with his son for becoming a Christian (*Letter* 276).[186] These trends continued in the Byzantine era. Ignatios, a ninth-century individual who held various religious posts, including that of metropolitan of Nicaea, bishop, monk, *skeuophylax* (keeper of religious vessels, furniture, and books), and deacon at Hagia Sophia, left sixty-four letters.[187] We can get some sense of his individual situation from these letters, but the standard epistolary functions are also readily identifiable.[188] In *Letter* 21, Ignatios writes to an official to put in a plea on behalf of the captains of the grain ships who transported grain for the Treasury. These men, acting under compulsion from hunger, had removed some of the wheat and made it up with barley and were facing severe punishment. In *Letter* 23, Ignatios complains that the official to whom he is writing has not assisted a widow who had previously put in a petition. To move forward to the late thirteenth and early fourteenth centuries, Athanasius I, Patriarch of Constantinople, in *Letter* 68, implores the emperor to put a stop to the cruelty of the tax collectors and not to deprive rent-payers of those established privileges on which they rely to feed their families. In

---

185 To give a pagan example, compare Symmachus, *Letter* 1.70, in which he asks his brother, Celsinus Titianus, *vicarius* of Africa, to help two men who were attempting to aid Eutychia, a woman of senatorial rank, and her dependents.

186 Compare Symmachus's *Letter* 1.55, which reveals that Praetextatus has offered to serve as a mediator between Symmachus and another individual.

187 Cyril Mango, ed. and trans., *The Correspondence of Ignatios the Deacon: Text, Translation, and Commentary*, with the collaboration of Stephanos Efthymiadis (Washington DC: Dumbarton Oaks Research Library and Collection, 1997), 1; 3; 5; 23.

188 His letters are taken up with property and money—the church's (*Letter* 1; 3; 6–8; 10; 17) or his own financial circumstances (*Letter* 39; 56).

*Letter* 99, he petitions for the needy; in *Letter* 106, he writes on behalf of those oppressed by grain-dealers and profiteers. The patriarch also uses letters to mediate between members of the imperial family (*Letter* 75; 85; 86; 97; 98).

A theme related to that of friendship is separation. Letter writers often lament their feelings of isolation, of being separated from their friends. Basil of Caesarea, in a letter to his friend, Eustathius the Philosopher, describes how he misses him both literally (since they are separated by such a great distance) and emotionally (*Letter* 1); Theophylact of Ochrid writes, "I have just set foot in Ochrid and I long for the city that holds you" (*Letter* G6, II, 147.2–3).[189] In the following example, we can see that such expressions are a convention of letter writing. Symmachus complains that his friend has reproached him without good reason (as a mere matter of form), as he has in fact been a frequent correspondent. "Admittedly an affectionate request for communication pleases the spirit, for even a complaint is sweet if it arises from fondness. But you should know that your insistence shows your correctness more than your reasonableness" (*Letter* 1.5.1).[190]

The letter was also an important medium of communication between bishops and their communities concerning proper doctrine, and a means of conducting doctrinal disputes. For example, Augustine, as well as various church councils and bishops, wrote many letters to laymen, to church officials, and to the pope in an attempt to refute and stamp out the Pelagians (*Letter* 157; 175–78; 181–83).[191] The bishops of Alexandria sent out

---

189  Trans. Mullet, *Theophylact of Ochrid*, 13; see Conybeare, *Paulinus Noster*, 60–90 on this theme in Christian letters.

190  Trans. Salzman, *Letters of Symmachus*, 23; for the Byzantine period see Mullet, "Classical Tradition," 79–80.

191  See also the letters exchanged between Augustine and Jerome, Augustine, *Letter* 166; 167 and Jerome, *Letter* 134; 141–43, which we discuss below.

annual "festal letters" to the congregations of Egypt, to inform them of the proper date of Easter. These could also include doctrinal matters, such as Athanasius's famous *Letter* 39, which delineates the biblical canon.

Imperial letters could be used to set an agenda or a tone for an emperor's reign, as when the emperor Julian exchanged letters with the philosopher Themistius, using the occasion to lay out his views on the proper relationship between philosophy and power.[192] When addressing an emperor via letter, the author generally displayed an awareness of the office, addressing the emperor in grandiose language, but the author could also betray an unexpected boldness. Through his letters, Bishop Ambrose tried to influence emperors on matters pertaining to public religion (*Letter* 17 and 18 on the altar of Victory; *Letter* 40 on the restoration of the Jewish synagogue). He asked for protection for various people or groups, such as in *Letter* 62, where he asks pardon for the followers of the defeated usurper Eugenius. He also provided Emperor Gratian with religious instruction in the form of treatises on theological topics (Letter of the Emperor Gratian to Ambrose; Ambrose, *Letter* 1, to the Emperor Gratian). Athanasius I, Patriarch of Constantinople, wrote many letters to the emperor or the imperial family and to various officials. His letters were probably put into a collection by his disciples soon after his death and date to the period after his first term as patriarch (1293–1303 CE) or to his second tenure (1303–1309 CE). Some show him exhorting the emperor to do his Christian duty:

> Again as so often I supplicate you, listen to my voice for the sake of Him Who made you emperor, Christ, God over all things. Rouse yourself to provide justice for the wronged, and punishment for sinners. Cleanse the Church from defilement, and do not refute the wickedness of schismatics with words alone …. In proportion therefore to their unyielding and

---

192 Discussed briefly above in Chapter 2; Elm, *Sons of Hellenism,* 80–87.

unrepentant hearts, let them taste the wrath of imperial judgement.¹⁹³

He was not adverse to asking for interventions on his own behalf, and in *Letter* 92, he sets himself up as proper counselor for the emperor: "It is for your divine majesty to refer everything after God to your spiritual father [Athanasius], to entrust undisguisedly to him whatsoever you rule whether on the left or right, to converse more frequently with him than with all other men, since 'the fit of the Holy Ghost' comes 'according to one's faith.' I entreat you to abound in this <spiritual wealth>, to pride yourself on it, and to adorn yourself with it."¹⁹⁴

Our survey of common themes between our two target periods has included Byzantine examples, but there were also some unique developments in the art of letter writing in this later period. What changed in the Byzantine period? is a question taken up by Margaret Mullet, in her essay, "Classical Tradition," and we draw primarily on her reconstruction in what follows.¹⁹⁵

In the Byzantine period, the divide between formal speech and writing and everyday speech and writing grew larger.¹⁹⁶ This led

---

193 Trans. Talbot, *Correspondence of Athanasius I*, 20; compare *Letter* 62, where describes himself as negligent, lazy, dissolute, and indolent, 147.

194 Trans. Talbot, *Correspondence of Athanasius I*, 241; for interventions for himself, see *Letter* 69; 78.

195 For a quick overview, see Margaret Mullet, "Epistolography," in *The Oxford Handbook of Byzantine Studies*, eds. Elizabeth Jeffries, John F. Haldon, and Robin Cormack (Oxford: Oxford University Press, 2008), 882–93; for an overview of scholarship on Byzantine letters, see Peter Hatlie, "Redeeming Byzantine Epistolography," *Byzantine and Modern Greek Studies* 20, no. 1 (1996): 213–48; for historical facts that we can cull from them, see A. Karpozelos, "Realia in Byzantine Epistolography X-XIIc," *Byzantinische Zeitschrift* 77, no. 1 (1984): 20–37; A. Karpozelos, "Realia in Byzantine Epistolography XIII—XVc," *Byzantinische Zeitschrift* 88, no. 1 (1995): 68–84.

196 Elizabeth Jeffreys, "Rhetoric in Byzantium," in *Companion to Greek Rhetoric*, ed. Ian Worthington (Malden, MA: Wiley-Blackwell, 2010), 168.

to a tendency that grew over time to write obscurely.[197] Obscurity (*asapheia*), or lack of clarity, became valued in Byzantine rhetoric and made its way into literary letters and can be seen especially clearly in tenth-century letters.[198]

Another trend in the Byzantine period was the fact that the relationship between the sender and recipient became the central focus; third parties were not given attention.[199] The form of address became increasingly important and also the inclusion of compliments to the recipient. These elements were calculated to indicate the relationship between sender and recipient.[200] Typical themes for the period included health, death, and the business of letter-writing itself (the act of composition or the act of sending or opening a letter).[201] Letter writers paid more attention to describing their own emotional state than they did to describing events going on in the larger world.[202] It was only much later, at the end of the Byzantine period, that letter writers began to show an interest in describing contemporary events. The letters of Demetrios Kydones (mid-fourteenth century CE) supply contemporary commentary on the plague, providing an indication

---

197 Littlewood, "'Ikon of the Soul,'" 209–12.

198 Margaret Mullett, "Writing in Early Medieval Byzantium," in *The Uses of Literacy in Early Medieval Europe*, ed. R. McKitterick (Cambridge: Cambridge University Press, 1989; repr., *Letters, Literacy and Literature in Byzantium*, Aldershot, UK/Burlington, VT: Ashgate, 2007), 178; George L. Kustas, *Studies in Byzantine Rhetoric* (Thessaloniki, 1973), 12; 63–100. This tendency remained in place through the eleventh and twelfth centuries. By the thirteenth century, the tendency was to be more descriptive: Mullet, "Classical Tradition," 87.

199 Mullet, "Classical Tradition," 82.

200 Mullet, "Classical Tradition," 78; for more on the address, see the detailed study by Michael Grünbart, *Formen der Anrede im byzantinischen Brief vom 6. bis zum 12. Jahrhundert. Wiener byzantinistische Studien*. Vol. 25 (Vienna: Verlag der österreichischen Akademie der Wissenschaften, 2005).

201 Mullet, "Classical Tradition," 79–81; on friendship in letters, see also Littlewood, "'Ikon of the Soul,'" 222.

202 Mullet, "Classical Tradition," 80; 82.

of the scale of death, its effect on the city of Constantinople, and the psychological effects on individuals.[203]

As an example of how understanding the rules of letter writing can help elucidate the history behind the text, we briefly take up *Letter* 28 in the collection of St. Augustine, a letter to St. Jerome, written in 394 or 395 CE. The letter begins in a typical fashion, with strong expressions of friendship, and ends with a reference to the letter carrier through whose means they will continue the conversation begun in this letter (1; 4). The opening section culminates in a request: Augustine asks Jerome to further the aims of the good brother Profuturus. Thus far, Augustine has followed the conventions of the letter of introduction.

But the letter is more than a simple letter of recommendation; Augustine goes on to explain that he feels impelled to go beyond the usual conventions.

> I ought perhaps to write no more, if I were willing to content myself with the style of a formal letter of introduction; but my mind overflows into conference with you, concerning the studies with which we are occupied in Christ Jesus our Lord, who is pleased to furnish us largely through your love with many benefits, and some helps by the way, in the path which He has pointed out to His followers. (1).

He refers to the work on textual variants of the Scriptures that Jerome has undertaken and is so bold as to offer Jerome a directive: "But I beseech you not to devote your labour to the work of translating into Latin the sacred canonical books, unless you

---

203 See for example *Letter* 179; 281; 316; for other subdivisions within the Byzantine tradition, see Mullet, "Epistolography," 886; Mullet, "Classical Tradition," 90–91, who notes that letters of the seventh through ninth centuries are full of political and religious themes and that letters of the eleventh and twelfth centuries show an interest in the themes of medicine, rhetoric, and exile (for those writing outside Constantinople, the cultural capital).

follow the method in which you have translated Job, viz. with the addition of notes, to let it be seen plainly what differences there are between this version of yours and that of the LXX [the Septuagint], whose authority is worthy of highest esteem," and seemingly challenges him on his philological work at points where there was disagreement: "if they were obscure, it is believed that you are as likely to have been mistaken as the others; if they were plain, it is not believed that they [the LXX] could possibly have been mistaken. Having stated the grounds of my perplexity, I appeal to your kindness to give me an answer regarding this matter" (2). In the following section, Augustine admonishes Jerome for what he perceives as an incorrect and dangerous interpretation of Galatians 2.11–14. Augustine accuses Jerome of thoughtlessly ascribing an intentional falsehood to Paul, thus opening the door to an "anything goes" approach to biblical exegesis, undermining the divine authority of the Scriptures. Augustine urges Jerome to apply himself and give "more thorough attention" to the text (3).

In comparing this letter to the models found in Pseudo-Demetrius, we might say that Augustine employs the techniques of the friendly letter, the commendatory letter, the admonishing letter, and the advisory letter. If we compare it to the style guide of Pseudo-Libanius/Pseudo-Proclus, it most resembles the "mixed" letter type. This is described in *Epistolary Styles* as comprising many styles (*Epistolary Styles* 45). The example that is given in *Epistolary Styles* of the mixed type both praises the recipient for his piety and learning, but also points out his errors. "I know that you live a life of piety, that you conduct yourself as a citizen in a manner worthy of respect, indeed, that you adorn the illustrious name of philosophy itself, with the excellence of an unassailable and pure citizenship. But in this one thing alone do you err, that you slander your friends. You must avoid that, for it is not fitting that philosophers engage in slander" (92).[204]

---

[204] Trans. Malherbe, *Ancient Epistolary Theorists*, 81.

To truly understand the dynamic between Augustine and Jerome, we must consider more than the influence of epistolary style guides. We must read *Letter* 28 against the background of their entire correspondence. We have seventeen of the letters exchanged between Augustine and Jerome.[205] Most of these letters are taken up with the criticism of Augustine on Jerome's interpretation of Galatians, as well as other criticisms, queries, and suggestions made by Augustine on Jerome's works. When he finally responds to Augustine, Jerome responds with anger. This leads Augustine to adopt a more conciliatory tone, but he never gives up his right, as he sees it, to question and to expect an answer. The theme of friendship, so common to Late Antique letters, runs throughout the exchange, but with a twist: Augustine repeatedly puts forward the argument that honest criticism must be allowed between friends and writes of "not only the affection but also the frankness due to friendship" (Augustine, *Letter* 82).[206]

The correspondence between the two men lasted for more than twenty-five years. This was partly due to some very ill luck. Letters repeatedly went astray and had to be rewritten and resent and Jerome had the unpleasant experience of having Augustine's criticisms of his exegetical strategy read and circulated in Rome before he ever saw them. But the most central issue is that, as Jennifer Ebbeler puts it, Augustine simply refused to play by the rules of the epistolary art. Ebbeler suggests that Jerome, an older, established theologian, would not have expected Augustine to write to him on terms of equality.[207]

---

205 Augustine, *Letter* 28; 40; 67; 71; 73; 82; 166; 167; Jerome, *Letter* 102; 103; 105; 112; 115; 134; 141–43. Carolinne White, *The Correspondence (394–419) between Jerome and Augustine of Hippo* (New York: Edwin Mellen Press 1990) places the letters in chronological order, providing translation and commentary.

206 Trans. White, *Correspondence*, 175.

207 Jennifer Ebbeler, "Mixed Messages: The Play of Epistolary Codes in Two Late Antique Latin Correspondences," in *Ancient Letters: Classical and Late Antique Epistolography*, eds. Ruth Morello and A.D. Morrison

Although by the end of their correspondence Augustine was a bishop, when he first wrote to Jerome, he had not yet risen in the ranks of the church, nor had he yet earned the reputation for literary and theological learning that he would later enjoy. The rules governing letter exchange in Late Antiquity included not only stylistic considerations, but also the fact that correspondents generally assumed "conventional personae," so that sender and recipient could be understood as student/teacher, doctor/patient, or father/son.[208] Augustine evokes a strongly negative response in Jerome when he assumes the top position in the hierarchical relationship between them, refusing to play the conventional role assigned to him, that of a young man consulting an older, wiser man.[209] Jerome consequently accuses Augustine of hubris and of attempting to make his reputation at Jerome's expense.[210] Augustine of course denies this, and there is no doubt that he was not in fact simply being captious or quibbling. The exegetical approach to Galatians 2.11–14 and the meaning to be extracted from the passage were part of larger debates that Augustine was having with Manicheans and Donastists; getting it right, he felt, was crucial.[211]

We may say that the entire correspondence is in fact not really about Jerome's approach to Scripture, but about Augustine's desire to combat heresy and to find an ally in that fight. Apart from the exchanges on Galatians, the remaining letters deal with the Pelagian heresy.[212] Jerome, although he never responds as quickly

---

(Oxford: Oxford University Press, 2007), 301–23. Compare Peter Brown, *Augustine of Hippo: A Biography, Revised Edition with a New Epilogue* (Berkeley: University of California Press, 2000), 271.

208 Ebbeler, "Mixed Messages," 302.
209 Ebbeler, "Mixed Messages," 315–23.
210 Jerome, *Letter* 105.
211 R. Cole-Turner, "Anti-Heretical Issues and the Debate Over Galatians 2.11–14 in the Letters of St. Augustine and St. Jerome," *Augustinian Studies* 11 (1980): 155–66.
212 White, trans., *Correspondence*, 7–10.

or as fully as Augustine would like him to, appears in the end to see Augustine as a colleague, a fellow champion of orthodoxy. In *Letter* 134, he writes, "I have decided to love you, welcome you, honour you, admire you and to defend your words as if they were my own .... Let us make a greater effort to eradicate that most dangerous heresy from the churches" and in *Letter* 141: "all the heretics hate you, and persecute me, too, with equal hatred."[213]

As we have seen in this brief survey, letter collections are good sources for the history of the social and intellectual life of elites, bishops and their congregations, emperors and religious officials, emperors and subjects, and doctrinal disputes in Late Antiquity and Byzantium. Although they were composed by intellectuals, members of the imperial administration, or members of the religious hierarchy, letter collections also contain information about groups lower on the social ladder. We have seen how the personality of individuals can come through the conventions of the genre, as in the case of Julian or Augustine; knowing these conventions helps us read these source types as an insider—as they would have been read and understood at the time.

---

213 White, trans., *Correspondence,* 227 and 230, respectively; compare Jerome, *Letter* 143.

CHAPTER 5
# Admonition and Exhortation

Late Antique and Byzantine sermons can be described as being "the same, but different." When one first begins to study them, it is perhaps the impression of the former that predominates. But soon will come the appreciation of how vibrant, how rich they are as sources. Nearly every sermon contains admonition and exhortation, but at the same time, sermons were delivered for many different occasions, and each was shaped to fit the specifics of its original delivery. Like the other source types covered so far in this book then, we should see the authors of sermons as working within a tradition, with the sermons being shaped by a set of expectations governing structure and content, but using that tradition to respond to a contemporary set of circumstances. And like our other focus types, they are good sources for many types of history, including social history, religious disputes, and relations between church and state and between state and society. They can sometimes provide information about specific historical events and peoples, but one of their most valuable uses is as a source for urban life. With so many of the extant sermons being delivered in cities, taken as whole, they give us the feel of city life and the function of the church within urban society. In what follows, we look at the function of sermons, what their authors thought they were supposed to be, and the themes and motifs of the sermons; we end the chapter by providing an illustrative example of a particular type of sermon, the funeral sermon.

In the fourth century CE, the common Latin term for sermon was *sermo,* but the words *tractare* or *tractatus* by this period also referred to sermons of all types. The word "homily" (*homilia*) has sometimes been differentiated from that of sermons (*logos; encomion*). Some have argued that homilies are really speeches or writings on specific books of the Bible, but the words sermon, exposition, and homily were used interchangeably in Late

Antiquity.[214] In the Byzantine period, however, there does appear to be some attempt at making a distinction between a sermon and a homily from the seventh century on, although it is difficult to create hard and fast definitions.[215]

There is evidence that sermons could be either circulated as a piece of writing or delivered orally. Most of what we cover in this chapter are sermons that were delivered orally.[216] But even when they were delivered orally, they could be written down for preservation and circulation. In Augustine, *Sermon* 352, it is made clear that Augustine had to devise a sermon on the spot. The lector had read the wrong passage, thus forcing Augustine to quickly readjust his prepared remarks, as we can see from his opening words: "It is the voice of the penitent that can be recognized in the words with which we responded to the singer of the Psalm: *Turn your face away from my sins, and blot out all my iniquities* (Ps 51:9). Since I hadn't prepared a sermon for your graces on this subject, I acknowledge that it is a command from the Lord that I should deal with it" (*Sermon* 352.1). In the *Life of Apa Aphou* 9, written at the close of fourth century, the saint asks to be shown a copy of a recently delivered sermon and wonders if the scribes could have made a mistake, thus indicating that he

---

214 Michele Pellegrino, "General Introduction," in Augustine, *Sermons I (1-19)*, trans. Michele Pellegrino, ed. John E. Rotelle (New York: New City Press, 2003), 13.

215 Mary B. Cunningham and Pauline Allen, "Introduction," in *Preacher and Audience: Studies in Early Christian and Byzantine Homiletics*, eds. Mary B. Cunningham and Pauline Allen (Leiden: Brill, 1998), 1-2.

216 For an example of a written sermon, see Ephraim of Syria, *On Admonition and Repentance* 21: "Thou to whom I have given the counsel of life, be not thou negligent in it. From that which is other men's (doctrine) have I written to thee; see thou despise not their words. And if I depart before thee, in thy prayer make mention of me. In every season pray and beseech that our love may continue true. But as for us, on behalf of these things let us offer up praise and honour to Father, to Son, and to Holy Spirit, now and for ever. Amen." Augustine, in *Retractions* 2.93.2, specifies that his letters "to the people" were dictated and his sermons were spoken.

too, had his sermons transcribed, moving them from oral performance to written text.[217] Moving further along in time, Photius the Byzantine patriarch had his sermons taken down by stenographers and calligraphers; according to his *Life*, Euthymius (patriarch 907–912 CE) copied out some of his own sermons and presented them to his monastery.[218]

Sermons of particularly high quality were distributed for imitation and for future communal reading. Caesarius of Arles wrote about the need to distribute the sermons of the fathers of old so that they could be read out by those who doubted their own abilities to preach effectively (*Sermon* 1.15). He created a book of sermons that he sent out to be copied and distributed. He exhorted presbyters and deacons to review it yearly and to read the sermons he sent to the people on major feast days, threatening them with the judgment of God if they should fail in this duty (*Sermon* 2; *Sermon* 3, preface). In the Byzantine period, sermons from Late Antique church fathers were still periodically read during church services. For example, the sermons of St. Basil were to be read on the Wednesday and Friday of Tyrophagy (Cheese-Week, that is the week preceding Lent in which dairy, fish, and eggs could be consumed, but not meat).[219]

Presbyters, bishops, and monks delivered sermons. Caesarius of Arles writes that any bishop, presbyter, or deacon could preach

---

217 As what was transcribed does not accord with correct doctrine.

218 Cyril Mango, *The Homilies of Photius Patriarch of Constantinople, English Translation, Introduction and Commentary* (Cambridge, MA: Harvard University Press, 1958), 8–9.

219 Mango, *Homilies of Photius Patriarch of Constantinople*, 221, citing Symeon of Thessalonica, *Responsa*, PG 155, cols. 904–05. The sermons of John Chyrsostom were also popular; see, for example, the *Rule* of the Monastery of St. John Stoudios 2, for the Paschal feast (*BMFD* 1:100) or the *Synaxrion of the Monastery of Theotokos Evergetis* T.53.5, on Palm Sunday: *The Synaxrion of the Monastery of Theotokos Evergetis: March–August, The Moveable Cycle*, text and trans. Robert Jordan (Belfast: Byzantine Enterprises, the Institute of Byzantine Studies, the Queen's University of Belfast, 2005), 455.

(*Sermon* 1.13). In sixth-century Byzantium, Eutychius the patriarch, Leontius the presbyter, and Constantine the deacon and archivist all preached.[220] Emperor Leo VI delivered several sermons for the celebration of various saints and religious feasts.[221] Sermons could be delivered in churches to the faithful, but could also be given before a restricted group, such as to a group of monastics or clergy members or to a select group inside the imperial palace. A clergyman did not have to preach strictly only in his hometown. Augustine for instance was asked to preach at other places besides Hippo (Possidius 7.1 and 9.1).

Preaching was done for regular, weekly services and for religious festivals. Sermons might also be delivered at the dedication of a new church or shrine. Sermons could even be made upon request. Caesarius of Arles in *Sermon* 233 states that the abbot, Arigius, asked him to address his community of monastics at Blanzac. Sermons could also be spoken or written for an urgent situation such as when John Chrysostom, who was then a presbyter, preached a series of sermons to the people of Antioch who were awaiting imperial judgment in the wake of their destruction of imperial statues. Theodore the Studite (c. 758–c. 826 CE) composed his Large and Small Catechesis to his monks in exile, to exhort them to keep to their rules and to stay strong in their time of persecution. Patriarch Nicholas I preached a sermon on the sack of Thessaloniki in 904 CE by the Arabs, in which he attributed the attack to the sins of the people and of himself.

In addition to these types, there were also funeral sermons, which took the form of eulogies but also still could contain admonitions and exhortations, or catechetical sermons, which

---

220 Pauline Allen, "The Sixth-Century Greek Homily: A Re-Assessment," in *Preacher and Audience*: *Studies in Early Christian and Byzantine Homiletics*, eds. Mary B. Cunningham and Pauline Allen (Leiden: Brill, 1998), 202–03 discusses their extant work.

221 Theodora Antonopoulou, *The Homilies of the Emperor Leo VI* (Leiden: Brill, 1997), 26–27.

were designed to deliver religious instruction to those joining the church.

Attendees came from all walks of life. In a Lenten sermon on the opening chapters of Genesis, Basil of Caesarea said: "I know that many artisans, belonging to mechanical trades, are crowding around me. A day's labour hardly suffices to maintain them; therefore I am compelled to abridge my discourse, so as not to keep them too long from their work" (*Hexæmeron* 3.1). To be intelligible to all was the goal. Peter Chrysologus, in a sermon on prayer, fasting, and almsgiving, asserted, "We should speak to the populace in popular fashion. The parish ought to be addressed by ordinary speech. Matters necessary to all men should be spoken about as men in general speak. Natural language is dear to simple souls and sweet to the learned. A teacher should speak words which will profit all. Therefore, today let the learned grant pardon for commonplace language" (*Sermon* 43).[222]

Yet some preachers spoke in a high rhetorical style in the Late Antique period, and it was commonplace to do so in the Byzantine era. In one of his sermons, Basil directly addresses "the more studious" of his auditors: "Perhaps many of you ask why there is such a long silence in the middle of the rapid rush of my discourse. The more studious among my auditors will not be ignorant of the reason why words fail me. What! Have I not seen them look at each other, and make signs to make me look at them, and to remind me of what I have passed over?" (*Hexæmeron* 8.2). Niki Tsironis suggests that rhetorical eloquence would not in fact be a hindrance to the uneducated as, through long familiarity, the conventions of the sermon would have helped to guide their understanding.[223]

---

222 Compare Caesarius of Arles: too much eloquence is counterproductive, as not everyone will be able to understand (*Sermon* 1.12), but rather priests "should preach to the people in simple, ordinary language which all the people can grasp" (*Sermon* 1.20).

223 Niki Tsironis, "Historicity and Poetry in Ninth-Century Homiletics: The

What was the intended function of the sermon? Augustine in *On Christian Doctrine* 4.4.6–7 provides an excellent summary.

> It is the duty, then, of the interpreter and teacher of Holy Scripture, the defender of the true faith and the opponent of error, both to teach what is right and to refute what is wrong, and in the performance of this task to conciliate the hostile, to rouse the careless, and to tell the ignorant both what is occurring at present and what is probable in the future. But once that his hearers are friendly, attentive, and ready to learn, whether he has found them so, or has himself made them so, the remaining objects are to be carried out in whatever way the case requires. If the hearers need teaching, the matter treated of must be made fully known by means of narrative. On the other hand, to clear up points that are doubtful requires reasoning and the exhibition of proof. If, however, the hearers require to be roused rather than instructed, in order that they may be diligent to do what they already know, and to bring their feelings into harmony with the truths they admit, greater vigor of speech is needed. Here entreaties and reproaches, exhortations and upbraidings, and all the other means of rousing the emotions, are necessary. And all the methods I have mentioned are constantly used by nearly every one in cases where speech is the agency employed.

Confirmation that Augustine here reflects a generally accepted idea of what a sermon was supposed to be is found in the fact that we see the topics reflected in this quote in numerous Late Antique sermons. Several other Late Antique authors also

---

Homilies of Patriarch Photios and George of Nicomedia," in *Preacher and Audience: Studies in Early Christian and Byzantine Homiletics*, eds. Mary B. Cunningham and Pauline Allen (Leiden: Brill, 1998), 306–09.

contain similar statements, as for instance in the writings of Bishop Ambrose (died 397 CE). In *Letter* 2.5, to Constantius, a newly appointed bishop, he wrote, "Let your discourses then be flowing, let them be clear and lucid; pour the sweetness of your moral arguments into the ears of the people, and sooth them with the charm of your words, that so they may willingly follow your guidance."[224]

Perhaps the most common element in sermons was the exhortation to live according to Christian virtues. Valerian, a fifth-century North African bishop, preached on discipline, the narrow way, watching one's tongue, and keeping one's vows. "But the proof of our conversion lies in this one fact, that we are good men" (*Homily* 1.7). Photius in *Homily* 2 states that he will try to emulate the great preachers who came before him in exhorting and teaching his congregation. "I shall perform my duty in exhorting you to what is needful, and inciting you to those deeds which are believed to keep our pact with God inviolate, which bring about victory over the Evil one, and yield the fruit of salvation in time of need" (1).[225] Isidore, Archbishop of Thessalonica (fourteenth century) directed his audience thusly: "To obtain, therefore, eternal life for yourself, hasten to practice the virtues for the love of God, wholeheartedly and perfectly. And in addition to this, love your neighbor as yourself" (*Homily* 3.2).[226]

Sermons were also vehicles for defending and explaining the correct interpretation of the Scriptures. Augustine's *Sermon* 51 takes up a potentially problematic issue with the gospel accounts of the genealogy of Christ. The real focus of the sermon

---

224  Translation by H. Walford, *The Letters of S. Ambrose, Bishop of Milan, Translated, with Notes and Indices* (Oxford: James Parker and Co., 1881), 6; see also Photius, *Homily* 2.

225  Translation by Mango, *Homilies of Photius*, 55.

226  Translation by Angela C. Hero, *Five Homilies of Isidore, Archbishop of Thessalonica: Edition, Translation and Commentary* (MA thesis, Columbia University, 1965), 290.

is to explain why the divine Christ was born of a human woman, a concept at which pagans and even some Christian groups balked. In 51.4ff, Augustine argues with imaginary disputants who try to disprove this central Christian belief by pointing to the seeming contradiction between the scriptural texts on the point of genealogy. Augustine demonstrates that although the evangelists Matthew and Luke appear to provide conflicting accounts, they are actually in harmony. His detailed exegesis provides his congregation with a model for how to respond should they be challenged on this topic.

Sermons also provided guidance on how to make converts. Caesarius of Arles describes how to make a pagan convert by relying on the argument from prophecy.

> The greater and older people of the Jews are proved to serve the younger, that is, the Christian people, for like servants of the Christians they are known to carry the books of the divine law throughout the world for the instruction of all nations. Therefore, the Jews were scattered in every land, so that when we want to invite some pagan to faith in Christ by testifying that Christ Himself was announced by all the prophets, and he resists and says that the holy books of the divine law were written by us rather than the Holy Ghost, we may thus have a means of refuting him with positive arguments. To such a man we may say: If a doubt arises in you concerning my books, behold the books of the Jews, apparently our enemies, which I certainly could neither have written nor changed. Read them over, and when you have found in them the same thing as in my books, 'Be not unbelieving, but believing.' [John 20.27] In this way the elder people is known to serve the younger, for through their books the people of the Gentiles are invited to belief in Christ." (*Sermon* 86)

## CHAPTER 5: ADMONITION AND EXHORTATION

Sermons were useful mediums for combating heresy. In a sermon by Gregory of Nazianzus, he lays out the beliefs of Eunomius, an Arian, and Macedonius, a Semi-Arian, and explains how a correct reading of Scripture disproves Arian doctrines.

> Since I have by the power of the Spirit sufficiently overthrown the subtleties and intricacies of the arguments, and already solved in the mass the objections and oppositions drawn from Holy Scripture, with which these sacrilegious robbers of the Bible and thieves of the sense of its contents draw over the multitude to their side, and confuse the way of truth .... Yet we have not yet gone through the passages in detail, because of the haste of our argument. But since you demand of us a brief explanation of each of them, that you may not be carried away by the plausibilities of their arguments, we will therefore state the explanations summarily, dividing them into numbers for the sake of carrying them more easily in mind. (*Oration* 30.1)

The sixth-century presbyter, Leontius, created imagined conversations with heretics in his sermons. "But Marathonius will say immediately ... But, Marathonius, who was it who spoke about Blessed Paul? ... Do you do away with Paul, Marathonius?" (9; 13).[227] The iconoclast sermons of John of Damascus and Theodore Studites are also good examples.

We can see from our discussion so far that there was a real attention to exegesis. Many sermons consisted largely of the preacher going through a biblical passage verse by verse to explain its meaning. "Such then is the general tenor of what is written after what we have previously examined; now would be the time to

---

227  Translation by Pauline Allen, *Fourteen Homilies, Translated, Introduced, and Annotated* by Pauline Allen with Cornelis Datema (Brisbane: Australian Association for Byzantine Studies, 1991), 160.

set out a word-by-word interpretation systematically, following the sequence of the words" (Gregory of Nyssa, *Homilies on Ecclesiastes* 2.307.15).[228] Alternative interpretations might be laid out and weighed. Archbishop Isidore, in a sermon on the man who, in traveling from Jerusalem to Jericho, was attacked by robbers and left for dead, provides an example:

> All our predecessors have expressed the view that, here, the word 'man' alludes to our forefather, Adam, and the word 'Jerusalem' to Paradise. They refer 'Jericho' to this world of ours, and the robbers to the demons or rather the latter's fatal counsel which has result in that most evil trespas .... The man was attacked by sin and passions .... I am in complete agreement with this interpretation developed by earlier authorities .... [But] [y]ou can also understand by the word 'man' the mind of each individual which, whenever it descends from Jerusalem to Jericho, that is to say, from the lofty and peaceful studies and occupations to the confusing cares of this world, falls right away into the hands of robbers, namely, the thoughts that strip it of its purity and close association with God. (*Homily* 3.3)[229]

In the following example, Hilary of Poitiers explains the difficult parts of the scriptural text in his *Homilies on Psalms* 1.21-22.

The terms of this utterance of the Lord are disturb-

---

228 Translation by Stuart George Hall and Rachel Moriarty in *Homilies on Ecclesiastes: An English Version with Supporting Studies: Proceedings of the Seventh International Colloquium on Gregory of Nyssa* (*St. Andrews, 5-10 September 1990*), ed. Stuart George Hall (Berlin: Walter de Gruyter, 1993), 54; Isidore, Archbishop of Thessalonica, *Homily* 4.8: "We have explained above how we must here understand the word, 'servant.' By considering, therefore, what has been said you will find the answer to anything that might puzzle you in this parable": trans. Hero, *Five Homilies of Isidore*, 345.

229 Trans. Hero, *Five Homilies of Isidore*, 294-95.

ing to inattentive hearers and careless, hasty readers. For by saying: *He that believeth on Me shall not be judged,* He exempts believers, and by adding: *But he that believeth not hath been judged already,* He excludes unbelievers, from judgment. If, then, He has thus exempted believers and debarred unbelievers, allowing the chance of judgment neither to one class nor the other, how can He be considered consistent when he adds thirdly: *And this is the judgment, that the light is come into the world, and men loved the darkness rather than the light*? For there can apparently be no place left for judgment, since neither believers nor unbelievers are to be judged. Such no doubt will be the conclusion drawn by inattentive hearers and hasty readers. The utterance, however, has an appropriate meaning and a rational interpretation of its own. He that believes, says Christ, is not judged. And is there any need to judge a believer? Judgment arises out of ambiguity, and where ambiguity ceases, there is no call for trial and judgment. Hence not even unbelievers need be judged, because there is no doubt about their being unbelievers; but after exempting believers and unbelievers alike from judgment, the Lord added a case for judgment and human agents upon whom it must be exercised. For some there are who stand midway between the godly and the ungodly, having affinities to both, but strictly belonging to neither class, because they have come to be what they are by a combination of the two.

A preacher might even take up textual variants or the meaning of specific Greek or Hebrew words.[230] Gregory of Nyssa stresses

---

230 On textual variants, see Basil, *Homilies on the Psalms* 13.1 [on Psalm 28] "In many copies we find added the words, 'Bring to the Lord, O ye children of God.' And, since indeed not everyone's gift is acceptable to God,

how necessary such exegesis is. In his introduction to *Homily* 1 on *Ecclesiastes*, he refers to the correct understanding of scripture as a laborious, intellectual exercise and notes that one has to be sure that one's interpretation is unassailable (1.277.3–279.3).[231]

We might not expect that congregations would be receptive to listening to detailed explanations of textual passages, but there is good evidence to suggest that they could be active participants. Although there are occasional complaints about lack of attention or attendance in the sources, there are just as many textual witnesses to the people's eager, fervent attention. Consider the example of Basil's *Hexæmeron* discussed above, in which he said: "Perhaps many of you ask why there is such a long silence in the middle of the rapid rush of my discourse. The more studious among my auditors will not be ignorant of the reason why words fail me. What! Have I not seen them look at each other, and make signs to make me look at them, and to remind me of what I have passed over?" (*Hexæmeron* 8.2)[232] In the conclusion to a

---

but only his who brings it with a pure heart, for Scripture says: 'The vows of a hired courtesan are not pure'; and again, Jeremia says: 'Shall not your vows and the holy flesh take away from you your crimes, or shall you be pure on account of these?' therefore, the psalm first wants us to be the children of God, then to seek to carry our gifts to God, and not just any gifts, but whatever ones He Himself has appointed"; on differences between the Hebrew and the LXX, see Jerome, *Homily* 61; on Greek meaning, see Hilary of Poitiers, *Homily on Psalm* 130(131).2.

231 God has commanded us to "search the scriptures" (Jn 5.39), and this the faithful must not fail to do (278.17).

232 On the congregation not attending sermons, see Gregory of Nazianzus, *Oration* 3.1: "How slow you are, my friends and brethren, to come to listen to my words." Mary Cunningham, "Dramatic Device or Didactic Tool? The Function of Dialogue in Byzantine Preaching," in *Rhetoric in Byzantium: Papers from the Thirty-fifth Spring Symposium of Byzantine Studies, Exeter College, University of Oxford, March 2001*, ed. Elizabeth Jeffreys (Aldershot, UK: Ashgate, 2003), 103; 112 cautions that interjections and questions in our extant sermons may simply be rhetorical devices on the part of the speaker (that is, he is pretending to respond to interjections). Cunningham also suggests that they may be understood as attempts on the part of a preacher to hold and keep the audience's

## CHAPTER 5: ADMONITION AND EXHORTATION

sermon on Zechariah, Peter Chrysologus stated: "I give thanks to my God who has seen to it that what I lost in speech I have gained in love. For how great your charity is towards me, your pallor revealed, your shouts bore witness, your tears manifested, and your abundant prayers made clear" (*Sermon* 86.7). When Gregory of Nazianzus returned to Constantinople after his rival had been vanquished, he attributed the zeal of the crowds to their love of his sermons (*Oration* 36.3).

John Chrysostom, in a homily concerning the power of demons, explicitly refers to the willingness of his audience to listen attentively to a very long sermon:

> Then accordingly—then ye shewed your insatiable longing. For when my discourse was extended to some length, yea to an interminable length, such as never was, many indeed expected that your eagerness would be quenched by the abundance of what was said. But the contrary happened. For your heart was the rather warmed, your desire was the rather kindled: and whence was this evident? The acclamations at least which took place at the end were greater, and the shouts more clear, and the same thing took place as at the forge. For as there at the beginning indeed the light of the fire is not very clear, but when the flame has caught the whole of the wood that is laid upon it, it is raised to a great height; so also accordingly this happened on the occasion of that day. (*Homilies Concerning the Power of Demons* 1.1)[233]

---

attention. If the latter is true, we might surmise that such methods were successful, since they were used in both the Late Antique and Byzantine periods.

233 Compare Basil, *Homilies on the Psalms* 20.1 [on Psalm 59] "When I compared the eagerness with which you listened and the inadequacy of my ability there came to my mind a certain similitude of a young child,

Earlier we noted that sermons from Late Antiquity continued to be read in the Byzantine period. For sermons composed in the Byzantine period, there were some stylistic changes. For one, although we have seen above that Augustine had already included imaginary disputants in his sermons, it was popular in some phases of the Byzantine period to include not only imagined conversations, but also imagined events related to biblical figures. Leontius's sermon on Job included imagined dialogues between Job and his friends, between Jesus and Judas, and between the Lord and the Devil (4.3–4, 7–8, 10–15). In a sermon on the Assumption, John of Damascus describes what happened when Mary the mother of Jesus died, how she was sent off to heaven, and her last moments on earth (*Sermon* 2), and Gregory Palamas explains how Mary was prepared to go into the Holy of Holies (*On the Entry of the Mother of God into the Holy of Holies I*).[234] Another notable change is that after the sixth century, there was a loss of topical references and the extant sermons appear to be mostly for festal occasions. These sermons seem to have been influenced by hymnography and had a "higher literary style and more rigid structure."[235] Mary Cunningham, who has studied

---

already rather active but not yet weaned from its mother's milk, annoying the maternal breasts which were dry from weakness. The mother, even though she perceived that the sources of her milk were dry, being pulled and torn by him, offered him her breast, not in order that she might nourish the infant, but that she might make him stop crying. Accordingly, even though our powers have been dried up by this long and varied bodily illness, nevertheless, there is set before you, not a pleasure deserving of mention, but some things which satisfy, because your extraordinary love is strong enough to appease your longing for us even by means of our voice alone." Photius also refers to his congregation's eagerness to hear him preach, even though it is on the same old theme, exhortation to virtue, that they had heard many times before (*Homily* 2).

234 St. John Damascene, *On Holy Images followed by Three Sermons on the Assumption*, trans. Mary H. Allies (London: Thomas Baker, 1898), 179–85; Gregory Palamas, *Mary the Mother of God: Sermons*, ed. Christopher Veniamin (South Canaan, PA: Mount Thabor Publishing, 2005), 8–15.

235 Mary Cunningham, "The Sixth-Century: A Turning-Point for Byzantine Homiletics?" in *The Sixth Century: End or Beginning?*, eds. Pauline

this change, cautions, however, that this may be due to the tastes of later-day compilers and preservers of our extant sermons.[236]

As historians today, what work do we think Late Antique and Byzantine sermons can do for us? As noted in the introduction to this chapter, due to the fact that many of our extant sermons were delivered in cities, much of what they have to tell us pertains to urban life. They provide us with biographical details; references to, and sometimes even descriptions of, historical events; and doctrinal conflicts. Late Antique sermons also speak to the role of bishops, other clergy, and monastics. For those interested in the shift from a pagan society to a Christian society, sermons provide much information about developing Christian views on wealth, slavery, education, marriage, and family life. They also compare and contrast pagan and Christian activities (pagan rites and festivals, attendance at the arena or the theater, use of enchantments, amulets, astrology). Sermons contain information relevant to the relationship between church and state, to biblical exegesis, and to the reading habits of Christians. They contain much by-the-way information about occupations and leisure activities.

For our last illustrative example, we take up a funeral sermon delivered by Theodore the Studite at the end of the eighth century (or beginning of the ninth) for his mother, Theoktiste, who was a monastic. The sermon is designated in the manuscript as a "funeral catechism." The funeral sermon is a derivative of a tradition of funeral speeches, which both Greek and Roman cultures had, though there was not a direct connection between the two in terms of their format.[237] A funeral speech did not have to be delivered immediately after death, but could be given months

---

Allen and Elizabeth Jeffreys (Leiden: Brill, 1996), 184.
236 Cunningham, "Sixth-Century," 185.
237 The Greek phrase for funeral speeches was *epitaphios logos*; Roman speeches of praise delivered at the funerals of great men were called *laudationes funebres*.

afterward. It resembled a panegyric in its contents. According to Menander Rhetor, the funeral speech, although it should have elements of consolation, is rightly considered an encomium (2.10.4). It should be comprised of all the usual encomiastic topics interspersed with brief statements of lament or consolation (2.10.5–8).

J.H.D. Scourfield has written on the elusiveness of the "consolation genre." As he points out, there were common themes but no one set literary format or medium through which consolation could properly be expressed.[238] And indeed we see that the funeral sermon by Theodore Studites shares many features in common with funeral speeches, but also with letters of consolation and saints' *Lives*. For example, Jerome wrote a letter of consolation to Eustochium on the death of her mother, Paula (*Letter* 108). Despite his insistence that the letter is not a panegyric (21), it follows many of the conventions of a conventional speech of praise, describing Paula's noble family connections both by birth and by marriage (3–4). The virtues for which she is praised have a distinctly Christian stamp, relating to her renunciation of wealth, worldly status, and family and to her knowledge of Scriptures (5–7; 15–19; 27). "If all the members of my body were to be converted into tongues, and if each of my limbs were to be gifted with a human voice, I could still do no justice to the virtues of the holy and venerable Paula. Noble in family, she was nobler still in holiness; rich formerly in this world's goods, she is now more distinguished by the poverty that she has embraced for Christ" (1).

The letter reads more like a eulogy or funeral speech than a letter, but Jerome himself describes the letter as a treatise (33). In format and content, the letter could just as well be considered a saint's *Life*. That there was overlap between letters and *Lives* is

---

[238] J.H.D. Scourfield, "Towards a Genre of Consolation," in *Greek and Roman Consolations: Eight Studies of a Tradition and Afterlife*, ed. Han Baltussen (Swansea: Classical Press of Wales, 2013), 1–36.

## CHAPTER 5: ADMONITION AND EXHORTATION

seen from that fact that some manuscripts of the *Life of Macrina*, written by her brother, Gregory of Nyssa, are in the form of a letter to the monk Olympios, although Gregory describes it as a *Life*.[239]

> As then you have decided that the story of her noble career is worth telling, to prevent such a life being unknown to our time, and the record of a woman who raised herself by 'philosophy' to the greatest height of human virtue passing into the shades of useless oblivion, I thought it well to obey you, and in a few words, as best I can, to tell her story in unstudied and simple style. (960B–C)[240]

Macrina's noble Christian parents, birth (complete with maternal prophetic vision), and exceptionally pious and studious childhood are the standard fare of *Lives*, and as seen in Chapter 2, reflect the guidelines for the imperial panegyric set out in Menander Rhetor's handbook. Like Paula, Macrina is praised for her renunciation of the world, her knowledge of Scriptures, and her leadership of her monastery. Her final moments and burial are described, as are the miracles and healings attributed to her.

Gregory of Nazianus delivered a funeral oration for his sister, Gorgonia. This he refers to as a speech of praise:

> In praising my sister, I shall pay honour to one of my own family; yet my praise will not be false, because it is given to a relation, but, because it is true, will be worthy of commendation, and its truth is based not

---

239 Carolinne White, *Lives of Roman Christian Women, Translated and Edited with an Introduction and Notes* (London, UK: Penguin, 2010), 21.
240 Translated by W.K. Lowther Clarke, *St. Gregory of Nyssa: Life of St. Macrina* (London: Society for Promoting Christian Knowledge, 1916), 18–19.

> only upon its justice, but upon well-known facts. For, even if I wished, I should not be permitted to be partial; since everyone who hears me stands, like a skilful critic, between my oration and the truth, to discountenance exaggeration, yet, if he be a man of justice, demanding what is really due. So that my fear is not of outrunning the truth, but, on the contrary, of falling short of it, and lessening her just repute by the extreme inadequacy of my panegyric. (1)

Further on, Gregory also describes his work as a eulogy (3). He begins with his sister's noble Christian parentage: "From them Gorgonia derived both her existence and her reputation; they sowed in her the seeds of piety" (6). Although married, she was able to devote herself wholly to God and to convince her whole family to do likewise (8). She is praised for her dedication to the Scriptures, charity, modesty, prudence, piety, and a simple lifestyle. Her last moments are described; she dies with a Psalm on her lips.

These works may be considered the literary predecessors of the funeral sermon of Theodore the Studite. Turning now to the funeral sermon itself, it begins much like any other sermon, with a focus on exhortation.

> Would you like me to tell you and all those present here ... of all the good and pious things, worthy of the kingdom of heaven, done by this blessed woman whilst she was alive? Then lend me your ears, my children, and I shall narrate everything to you, removed from all falsehood; and this narration concerning her shall be unto you even as an instruction in faith, nor one lacking in reason, but indeed most beneficial. (1)[241]

---

241 Translated by J.M. Featherstone in Stephanos Efthymiadis and J.M. Featherstone, "Establishing a Holy Lineage: Theodore the Studite's

## CHAPTER 5: ADMONITION AND EXHORTATION

A narrative account is given of her life, in which we see the usual *topoi* of saints' *Lives*. Theodore's mother had a keen dedication to the Scriptures, teaching herself to read at night (3; 11). She waited on the poor with her own hands and took out loans to help others pay off theirs; she made clothes for the monastery (11). Going one better than Gorgonia, she convinced her family to join her in a monastic life (6).

One might well wonder how much of this description is real: when the funeral sermon is presented back to back with earlier, similar works, one cannot help but suspect the intention of the speaker. Is it the speaker's intention to provide a true and accurate account of his mother's life story? There are some unusual features in Theoktiste's narrative. Whereas Paula (Jerome, *Letter* 108.20) corrected her nuns by severe looks, verbal reprimands, or, in extreme cases, isolation, the mother of Theodore Studites preferred a more physical approach:

> If one is to find fault with her, as with any human being, the reasons for this stem from her same fervor for the good, intense as she most often was in her instructions to the monastic women in obedience to her. For at times she grew angry because of faults either in the performance of tasks or psalm-singing or standing during the offices; so much so, that sometimes she could not refrain from giving a push to those who were nodding off or striking those who disobeyed. (12)[242]

---

Funerary Catechism for His Mother (BHG 2422)," in *Theatron: Rhetorische Kultur in Spätantike und Mittelalter/Rhetorical Culture in Late Antiquity and the Middle Ages*, ed. M. Grünbart (Berlin: Walter de Gruyter, 2007), 13–51, with introduction, edition, and annotation by Stephanos Efthymiadis; translation by Featherstone (42–51).

242 Trans. Featherstone, "Establishing a Holy Lineage," 49; on uncovering the woman behind the sermon, see Efthymiadis, "Establishing a Holy Lineage," 17–20, who identifies in Theodore's description of Theoktiste several points of departures from the ideal holy woman.

This uncontrollable temper appears to have been a holdover from her pre-monastic days, as earlier in the sermon, her son had revealed that she had also showed a tendency to slap her servants (5). Such personal details have the ring of truth, and we appear to get the same in the descriptions of her conflict with other monastics and the emperor and her propensity for travel (8–11).

The sermon tells us that Theodore, his mother, and the people present on the occasion of the sermon, still valued the ideals of the Late Antique Christian female saint: a woman who was prepared to renounce the world and live out her days devoted to charity, asceticism, and Scripture. But it also reveals to us a unique individual, a real, flesh and blood person, who had a particular set of both good and bad qualities. The lens of Christian encomium through which she was viewed by Theodore was the lens through which she would have viewed herself, and it is therefore the perspective with which we, as historians, must start. We can today, of course, then go on to approach the life of Theoktiste from other angles and attempt to view her life through multiple lenses, but step one is to take the past on its own terms and understand how the people of the past saw themselves. Understanding the close connection between form and content or between a society's values and the expression of those values in literary form—in the shape of standard genres—helps us to do that.

This chapter has described in summary fashion the function of the sermon in Late Antique and Byzantine society, the characteristic types of sermon, and broad changes in the style of sermons across these two periods. As the above examples have shown, when approaching a sermon as a historical source, the first step is to ask what type of sermon it is and to compare it to other examples of that sermon type. Given the genre and the stylistic fashions of the time, what can the reader expect to find in it? Imagined dialogues or an extended refutation of the Pelagian heresy?

## CHAPTER 5: ADMONITION AND EXHORTATION

Sermons were an important means of communication between members of the religious hierarchy and the laity. They were a medium that worked across class lines, as sermons were delivered to emperors and commoners alike. With weekly sermons, special liturgical sermons, and sermons for significant events in the city or an individual's life, they would have been a constant in the life of the average citizen.

## CHAPTER 6
# Conclusion

This brief survey of some of the most prominent literary forms of Late Antiquity and Byzantium has hopefully demonstrated the value of studying genre. When attempting to draw on a letter, a legal text, a code of conduct, a sermon, a speech of praise, or a *Life*, the student of history should be familiar with the usual formats and themes of that genre. The historian should also have in mind how that type of writing functioned within the larger society. Was it intended to inspire? To admonish? To honor? Was it part of an attempt to build up a community or to build up an individual's personal reputation? Perhaps it may be both! Genres were flexible, they did not keep to one rigid form, and these literary works tended to play more than one role in Late Antique and Byzantine societies. This makes their utilization as historical sources messy, but it also makes them all the more valuable: we can derive not only concrete historical details, the *orbiter dicta* of life in antiquity scattered here and there throughout the texts, but we can also use these literary forms as windows into the ideology and social norms of their times.

Generalizations, like comparisons, are odious, but overall it is fair to say that the primary aim of the authors of our focus genres was not to accurately reflect what was happening in the present or what had happened in the past. But this was understood by their intended audience. Understanding the intention behind these texts, what led to their development, and the part they played in their societies opens up the world of Late Antiquity and Byzantium to us in a way that consulting the historical narratives alone cannot. These sources give us insight into both public life and private life and into the world of government administration, but also into the communal life of the church and guideposts for personal piety. Composed by educated elites, these source types were not confined to that milieu; laws, letters, sermons, and panegyrics were part of everyday life for all classes of persons.

## TRANSLATIONS

Ambrose. *The Letters of S. Ambrose, Bishop of Milan*. Translated, with Notes and Indices by H. Walford. Oxford: James Parker and Co., 1881.

Ammianus Marcellinus. *History*. Vol. 1, *Books 14–19*. Translated by J. C. Rolfe. Loeb Classical Library 300. Cambridge, MA: Harvard University Press, 1950.

*Apostolic Constitutions*. Book VIII. Translated by James Donaldson. From *Ante-Nicene Fathers*, Vol. 7. Edited by Alexander Roberts, James Donaldson, and A. Cleveland Coxe. Buffalo, NY: Christian Literature Publishing Co., 1886.

*The Apostolical Constitutions; or, Canons of the Apostles, in Coptic*. Translated by Henry Tattam. London, UK: Printed for the Oriental translation fund of Great Britain and Ireland, 1848.

Athanasius I. *The Correspondence of Athanasius I, Patriarch of Constantinople: Letters to the Emperor Andronicus II, Members of the Imperial Family, and Officials*. Edition, Translation, and Commentary by Alice-Mary Maffry Talbot. Washington, DC: Dumbarton Oaks Center for Byzantine Studies, 1975.

Augustine. *On Christian Doctrine*. Translated by James Shaw. In *Nicene and Post Nicene Fathers, First Series*, Vol. 2. Edited by Philip Schaff. Buffalo, NY: Christian Literature Publishing Company, 1887.

Augustine. *Letter* 28. Translated by J.G. Cunningham. In *Nicene and Post-Nicene Fathers, First Series*, Vol. 1. Edited by Philip Schaff. Buffalo, NY: Christian Literature Publishing Co., 1887.

Augustine. *Letter* 82. Translated by Carolinne White. In *The Correspondence (394–419) between Jerome and Augustine of Hippo*. New York: Edwin Mellen Press 1990.

Augustine. *Letters 1–99.* Vol. II/1. Translation and Notes by Roland Teske. Edited by John E. Rotelle. New York: New City Press, 2001.

Augustine. *Sermons (341–400) on Various Subjects.* Vol. III/10. Translation and Notes by Edmund Hill. Edited by John E. Rotelle. New York: New City Press, 1995.

Basil. *Hexæmeron.* Translated by Blomfield Jackson. In *Nicene and Post Nicene Fathers, Second Series.* Vol. 8. Edited by Philip Schaff and Henry Wace. Edinburgh: T & T Clark, 1895.

Basil. *Exegetic Homilies.* Translated by Agnes Clare Way. Washington, DC: The Catholic University of America Press, 1963.

Caesarius of Arles. *Sermons.* Vol. 1 *(1–80).* Translated by Mary Magdeleine Mueller. Washington, DC: The Catholic University of America Press, 1956.

Caesarius of Arles. *Sermons. Volume II (81–186).* Translated by Mary Magdeleine Mueller. Washington, DC: The Catholic University of America Press, 1964.

Ephraim of Syria. "Three Homilies." Translated by A. Edward Johnston. In *Nicene and Post Nicene Fathers, Second Series*, Vol. 13, Part 2. Edited by Philip Schaff and Henry Wace, 305–41. Edinburgh: T & T Clark, 1898.

John Chrysostom. "Three Homilies Concerning the Power of Demons." Translated by T. P. Brandram. In *Nicene and Post-Nicene Fathers, First Series*, Vol. 9. Edited by Philip Schaff. Edinburgh: T & T Clark, 1889.

Claudius Mamertinus. "Speech of Thanks to Julian." Translated by Marna M. Morgan. In *The Emperor Julian: Panegyric and Polemic: Claudius Mamertinus, John Chrysostom, Ephrem the*

*Syrian*. Edited by Samuel N.C. Lieu, 13–38. Liverpool: Liverpool University Press, 1986.

*Codex* of Justinian. Translated by S.P. Scott, editor. *The Civil Law: Including the Twelve Tables, the Institutes of Gaius, the Rules of Ulpian, the Opinions of Paulus, the Enactments of Justinian, and the Constitutions of Leo*. Cincinnati: Central Trust Co., 1932. Reprint, New York: AMS Press, 1973.

[Demetrius of Phalerum]. *Epistolary Types*. Translated by Abraham J. Malherbe. In *Ancient Epistolary Theorists*. Atlanta, GA: Scholars Press, 1988.

*Didascalia Apostolorum*. Translated by R. Hugh Connolly. Oxford: Clarendon Press, 1929.

*Digest*. "The Composition of the *Digest*." Translated by Alan Watson. In *The Digest of Justinian*. Vol. I. Philadelphia: University of Pennsylvania, 1985.

*Ecloga*. Translated by Edwin Hanson Freshfield. In *Roman Law in the Later Roman Empire*: *The Isaurian Period, Eighth Century, the* Ecloga. Cambridge, UK: Bowes & Bowes, 1932.

*Eisagoge*. "The Prooimion of the Eisagoge." Translation and Commentary by W.J. Aerts, T.E. van Bochove, M.A. Harder, A. Hilhorst, J.H.A. Lokin, R. Meijering, S.L. Radt, J. Roldanus, B.H. Stolte, and N. van der Wal. Edited by B.H. Stolte and R. Meijering. *Subseciva Groningana*: *Studies in Roman and Byzantine Law* 7 (2001): 91–155.

Eusebius. "Church History." Translated by Arthur Cushman McGiffert. In *Nicene and Post-Nicene Fathers, Second Series*, Vol. 1. Edited by Philip Schaff and Henry Wace. Edinburgh: T & T Clark, 1890.

Gregory the Cellarer. *Life of St. Lazaros*. *The Life of Lazaros of Mt. Galesion*: *An Eleventh Century Pillar Saint*. Introduction,

Translation, and Notes by Richard P.H. Greenfield. Washington, DC: Dumbarton Oaks Research Library and Collection, 2000.

Gregory of Nazianzus. "Select Orations." Translated by Charles Gordon Browne and James Edward Swallow. In *Nicene and Post-Nicene Fathers, Second Series*. Vol. 7. Edited by Philip Schaff and Henry Wace. Edinburgh: T & T Clark, 1894.

Gregory of Nyssa. *Homilies on Ecclesiastes: An English Version with Supporting Studies: Proceedings of the Seventh International Colloquium on Gregory of Nyssa (St. Andrews, 5–10 September 1990)*. Edited by Stuart George Hall. Translation by Stuart George Hall and Rachel Moriarty, 31–144. Berlin: Walter de Gruyter, 1993.

Gregory of Nyssa. "Life of Macrina." Translated by W.K. Lowther Clarke. In *St. Gregory of Nyssa: Life of St. Macrina*. London: Society for Promoting Christian Knowledge, 1916.

Gregory Palamas. *Mary the Mother of God: Sermons*. Edited by Christopher Veniamin. South Canaan, PA: Mount Thabor Publishing, 2005.

Gregory of Tours. *Life of the Fathers*. Translated by Edward James. 2nd ed. Liverpool: Liverpool University Press, 1991.

Hilary of Poitiers. "Homilies on Psalms." Translated by E.W. Watson and L. Pullan. In *Nicene and Post-Nicene Fathers, Second Series*. Vol. 9. Edited by Philip Schaff and Henry Wace. Edinburgh: T & T Clark, 1898.

Ignatios the Deacon. *The Correspondence of Ignatios the Deacon: Text, Translation, and Commentary* by Cyril Mango, with the collaboration of Stephanos Efthymiadis. Washington DC: Dumbarton Oaks Research Library and Collection, 1997.

Isidore, Archbishop of Thessalonica. *Five Homilies of Isidore, Archbishop of Thessalonica*. Edition, Translation, and Commentary by Angela C. Hero. MA Thesis, Columbia University, 1965.

Jerome. "Letter 108." Translated by W.H. Fremantle, G. Lewis and W.G. Martley. From Nicene and Post-Nicene Fathers, Second Series, Vol. 6. Edited by Philip Schaff and Henry Wace. Buffalo, NY: Christian Literature Publishing Co., 1892.

Jerome. "Letter 134." Translated by Carolinne White. In *The Correspondence (394–419) between Jerome and Augustine of Hippo*. New York: Edwin Mellen Press 1990.

John Chrysostom. "Three Homilies Concerning the Power of Demons." Translated by T.P. Brandram. In *From Nicene and Post-Nicene Fathers, First Series*. Vol. 9. Edited by Philip Schaff. Edinburgh: T & T Clark, 1889.

John Damascene. *On Holy Images Followed by Three Sermons on the Assumption*. Translated by Mary H. Allies. London, UK: Thomas Baker, 1898.

Julian. *Orations 1–5*. Translated by Wilmer C. Wright. Loeb Classical Library 13. Cambridge, MA: Harvard University Press, 1913.

Julian. *Orations 6–8. Letters to Themistius, To the Senate and People of Athens, To a Priest. The Caesars. Misopogon*. Translated by Wilmer C. Wright. Loeb Classical Library 29. Cambridge, MA: Harvard University Press, 1913.

Leontius the presbyter. *Fourteen Homilies*. Translated, Introduced, and Annotated by Pauline Allen with Cornelis Datema. Brisbane: Australian Association for Byzantine Studies, 1991.

Libanius. *Selected Letters of Libanius from the Age of Constantius and Julian*. Translated by Scott Bradbury. Liverpool: Liverpool University Press, 2004.

Libanius. *Selected Orations*. Vol. 1, *Julianic Orations*. Edited and translated by A.F. Norman. Loeb Classical Library 451. Cambridge, MA: Harvard University Press, 1969.

Menander Rhetor, Dionysius of Halicarnassus. *Menander Rhetor. Dionysius of Halicarnassus, Ars Rhetorica*. Edited and translated by William H. Race. Loeb Classical Library 539. Cambridge, MA: Harvard University Press, 2019.

*Novels* of Justinian. Translated by S.P. Scott, ed. *The Civil Law: Including the Twelve Tables, the Institutes of Gaius, the Rules of Ulpian, the Opinions of Paulus, the Enactments of Justinian, and the Constitutions of Leo*. Cincinnati: Central Trust Co., 1932. Reprint, New York: AMS Press, 1973.

Peter Chrysologus. "Sermon 43." Translated by George E. Ganss. In *Saint Peter Chrysologus Selected Sermons and Saint Valerian Homilies*. Washington, DC: The Catholic University of America Press, 1953.

Peter Chrysologus. *Sermon* 86. Translated by William B. Palardy. In *Saint Peter Chrysologus Selected Sermons*. Vol. 3. Washington, DC: The Catholic University of America Press, 2005.

Photius. *The Homilies of Photius Patriarch of Constantinople*. English Translation, Introduction, and Commentary by Cyril Mango. Cambridge, MA: Harvard University Press, 1958.

Shenoute. "Let Our Eyes." Translated by Stephen Emmel. In *Selected Discourses of Shenoute the Great: Community, Theology, and Social Conflict in Late Antique Egypt*. Translated with introductions by David Brake and Andrew Crislip, 206–11. Cambridge, UK: Cambridge University Press, 2015.

Sidonius Apollonarius. *The Letters of Sidonius*. Translated, with Introduction and Notes by O.M. Dalton. Oxford: Clarendon Press, 1915.

Symmachus. *The Letters of Symmachus: Book 1*. Translation by

Michele Renee Salzman and Michael Roberts, with General Introduction and Commentary by Michele Renee Salzman. Atlanta: Society of Biblical Literature, 2011.

Theodore the Studite. *Funerary Catechism for His Mother*. Translated by J.M. Featherstone in Stephanos Efthymiadis and J.M. Featherstone, "Establishing a Holy Lineage: Theodore the Studite's Funerary Catechism for His Mother (BHG 2422)." In *Theatron: Rhetorische Kultur in Spätantike und Mittelalter/ Rhetorical Culture in Late Antiquity and the Middle Ages*. Edited by M. Grünbart, 13–51. Berlin: Walter de Gruyter, 2007.

*The Theodosian Code and Novels, and the Sirmondian Constitutions*. A Translation with Commentary, Glossary, and Bibliography by Clyde Pharr, in collaboration with Theresa Sherrer Davidson and Mary Brown Pharr; with an Introduction by C. Dickerman Williams. Princeton, NJ: Princeton University Press, 1952.

Quintilian. *The Orator's Education, Books I-III*. Translated by H.E. Butler. Loeb Classical Library. Cambridge, MA: Harvard University Press, 1920.

Valerian. *Homily* 1. Translated by George E. Ganss. In *Saint Peter Chrysologus Selected Sermons and Saint Valerian Homilies*. Washington, DC: The Catholic University of America Press, 1953.

# Bibliography

Allen, Pauline. "The Sixth-Century Greek Homily: A Reassessment." In *Preacher and Audience: Studies in Early Christian and Byzantine Homiletics*. Edited by Mary B. Cunningham and Pauline Allen, 201–25. Leiden: Brill, 1998.

Allen, Pauline. "Rationales for Episcopal Letter-Collections in Late Antiquity." In *Collecting Early Christian Letters: From the Apostle Paul to Late Antiquity*. Edited by Bronwen Neil and Pauline Allen, 18–34. Cambridge, UK: Cambridge University Press, 2015.

Angelov, Dimiter G. "Byzantine Imperial Panegyric as Advice Literature (1204–c. 1350)." In *Rhetoric in Byzantium: Papers from the Thirty-fifth Spring Symposium of Byzantine Studies, Exeter College, University of Oxford, March 2001*. Edited by Elizabeth Jeffreys, 55–72. Aldershot, UK: Ashgate, 2003.

Anderson, Graham. *Sage, Saint and Sophist: Holy Men and Their Associates in the Early Roman Empire*. New York: Routledge, 1994.

Antonopoulou, Theodora. *The Homilies of the Emperor Leo VI*. Leiden: Brill, 1997.

Baldovin, John F. "Hippolytus and the *Apostolic Tradition*: Recent Research and Commentary." *Theological Studies* 64 (2003): 520–42.

Bell, David N. *The Life of Shenoute by Besa: Introduction, Translation, and Notes*. Kalamazoo, MI: Cistercian Publications, 1983.

Blumell, Lincoln H. and Thomas A. Wayment, eds. *Christian Oxyrhynchus: Texts, Documents, and Sources*. Waco, TX: Baylor University Press, 2015.

Bradshaw, Paul F., Maxwell E. Johnson, and L. Edward Phillips. *The Apostolic Tradition: A Commentary*. Edited by Harold W. Attridge. Minneapolis, MN: Fortress Press, 2002.

Brakke, David and Andrew Crislip. *Selected Discourses of Shenoute the Great: Community, Theology, and Social Conflict in Late Antique Egypt*. Translated with Introductions. Cambridge, UK: Cambridge University Press, 2015.

Brown, Peter. *Augustine of Hippo: A Biography, Revised Edition with a New Epilogue*. Berkeley: University of California Press, 2000.

Cameron, Averil. *Christianity and the Rhetoric of Empire: The Development of Christian Discourse*. Berkeley: University of California Press, 1992.

———. "Form and Meaning: The *Vita Constantini* and the *Vita Antonii*." In *Greek Biography and Panegyric in Late Antiquity*. Edited by Tomas Hägg and Philip Rousseau, 72–88. Berkeley: University of California Press, 2000.

Chitwood, Zachary. *Byzantine Legal Culture and the Roman Legal Tradition, 867–1056*. Cambridge, UK: Cambridge University Press, 2017.

Clark, Gillian. "Philosophic Lives and the Philosophic Life: Porphyry and Iamblichus." In *Greek Biography and Panegyric in Late Antiquity*. Edited by Tomas Hägg and Philip Rousseau, 29–51. Berkeley: University of California Press, 2000.

———. *Women in Late Antiquity: Pagan and Christian Lifestyles*. Oxford: Oxford University Press, 1994.

Cole-Turner, R. "Anti-heretical Issues and the Debate Over Galatians 2.11–14 in the Letters of St. Augustine and St. Jerome." *Augustinian Studies* 11 (1980): 155–66.

Conybeare, Catherine. *Paulinus Noster: Self and Symbols in the Letters of Paulinus of Nola*. Oxford: Oxford University Press, 2000.

Constable, Giles. "Preface." In *Byzantine Monastic Foundation Documents: A Complete Translations of the Surviving Founders' Typika and Testaments*. Vol. 1. Edited by John Thomas and Angela Constantinides, with the assistance of Giles Constable, xi–xxxvii. Washington, DC: Dumbarton Oaks Research Library and Collection, 2000.

Coon, Lynda L. *Sacred Fictions: Holy Women and Hagiography in Late Antiquity*. Philadelphia: University of Pennsylvania Press, 1997.

Cox, Patricia. *Biography in Late Antiquity: A Quest for the Holy Man*. Berkeley: University of California Press, 1983. (See also Patricia Cox Miller)

Cunningham, Mary. "Dramatic Device or Didactic Tool? The Function of Dialogue in Byzantine Preaching." In *Rhetoric in Byzantium: Papers from the Thirty-fifth Spring Symposium of Byzantine Studies, Exeter College, University of Oxford, March 2001*. Edited by Elizabeth Jeffreys, 101–13. Aldershot, UK: Ashgate, 2003.

———. "The Sixth-Century: A Turning-Point for Byzantine Homiletics?" In *The Sixth Century: End or Beginning?* Edited by Pauline Allen and Elizabeth Jeffreys, 176–86. Leiden: Brill, 1996.

Cunningham, Mary and Pauline Allen. "Introduction." In *Preacher and Audience: Studies in Early Christian and Byzantine Homiletics*. Edited by Mary B. Cunningham and Pauline Allen, 1–20. Leiden: Brill, 1998.

Dennis, G.T. "Imperial Panegyric: Rhetoric and Reality." In *Byzantine Court Culture from 829 to 1204*. Edited by Henry

Maguire, 131–40. Washington, DC: Dumbarton Oaks Research Library and Collection, 1997.

Drake, H.A. *In Praise of Constantine: A Historical Study and New Translation of Eusebius' Tricennial Orations*. Berkeley: University of California Press, 1976.

Ebbeler, Jennifer. "Mixed Messages: The Play of Epistolary Codes in Two Late Antique Latin Correspondences." In *Ancient Letters: Classical and Late Antique Epistolography*. Edited by Ruth Morello and A.D. Morrison, 301–23. Oxford: Oxford University Press, 2007.

Efthymiadis, Stephanos, ed. *Ashgate Research Companion to Byzantine Hagiography*. Vol. 1, *Periods and Places*. Farnham, UK/Burlington, VT: Ashgate, 2011.

———. ed. *The Ashgate Research Companion to Byzantine Hagiography*. Vol. 2, *Genres and Contexts*. Farnham, UK/Burlington, VT: Ashgate, 2014.

———. "The Byzantine Hagiographer and His Audience in the Ninth and Tenth Centuries." In *Metaphrasis: Redactions and Audiences in Middle Byzantine Hagiography*. Edited by Christian Høgel, 59-80. Oslo: The Research Council of Norway, 1996.

Efthymiadis, Stephanos and J.M. Featherstone. "Establishing a Holy Lineage: Theodore the Studite's Funerary Catechism for His Mother (BHG 2422)." In *Theatron: Rhetorische Kultur in Spätantike und Mittelalter/Rhetorical Culture in Late Antiquity and the Middle Ages*. Edited by M. Grünbart, 13–51. Berlin: Walter de Gruyter, 2007.

Efthymiadis, Stephanos and Nikos Kalogeras. "Audience, Language and Patronage in Byzantine Hagiography." In *Ashgate Research Companion to Byzantine Hagiography*. Vol. 2, *Genres and Contexts*. Edited by Stephanos Efthymiadis, 247–84. Farnham/Burlington, VT: Ashgate, 2014.

Elm, Susanna. *Sons of Hellenism, Fathers of the Church: Emperor Julian, Gregory of Nazianzus, and the Vision of Rome*. Berkeley: University of California, 2012.

Fögen, Marie Theres. "Legislation in Byzantium: A Political and a Bureaucratic Technique." In *Law and Society in Byzantium, Ninth-Twelfth Centuries*. Edited by Angeliki E. Laiou and Dieter Simon, 53–70. Washington, DC: Dumbarton Oaks Research Library and Collection, 1994.

Goehring, James E. "The Encroaching Desert: Literary Production and Ascetic Space in Early Christian Egypt." *Journal of Early Christian Studies* 1, no. 3 (1993): 281–96. Reprint, *Ascetics, Society, and the Desert: Studies in Early Egyptian Monasticism*, 73–88. Harrisburg, PA: Trinity Press, 1999.

Grünbart, Michael. *Formen der Anrede im byzantinischen Brief vom 6. bis zum 12. Jahrhundert. Wiener byzantinistische Studien*. Vol. 25. Vienna: Verlag der österreichischen Akademie der Wissenschaften, 2005.

Hägg, Tomas and Philip Rousseau. "Introduction: Biography and Panegyric." In *Greek Biography and Panegyric in Late Antiquity*. Edited by Tomas Hägg and Philip Rousseau, 1–28. Berkeley: University of California Press, 2000.

Harries, Jill. "Introduction: The Background to the Code." In *The Theodosian Code: Studies in the Imperial Law of Late Antiquity*. Edited by Jill Harries and Ian Wood, 1–16. Ithaca, NY: Cornell University Press, 1993.

———. *Law and Empire in Late Antiquity*. Cambridge, UK: Cambridge University Press, 1999.

———. "Resolving Disputes: The Frontiers of Law in Late Antiquity." In *Law, Society and Authority in Late Antiquity*. Edited by Ralph W. Mathisen, 68–82. Oxford: Oxford University Press, 2001.

Hatlie, Peter. "Redeeming Byzantine Epistolography." *Byzantine and Modern Greek Studies* 20, no. 1 (1996): 213–48.

Honoré, Tony. "The Making of the Theodosian Code." *Zeitschrift der Savigny-Stiftung für Rechtsgeschichte. Romanistische Abteilung* 103 (1986): 133–222.

———. "Some Quaestors of the Reign of Theodosius II." In *The Theodosian Code: Studies in the Imperial Law of Late Antiquity*. Edited by Jill Harries and Ian Wood, 68–93. Ithaca, NY: Cornell University Press, 1993.

Humfress, Caroline. "Law and Legal Practice in the Age of Justinian." In *The Cambridge Companion to the Age of Justinian*. Edited by Michael Maas, 161–84. Cambridge, UK: Cambridge University Press, 2005.

———. "Law in Practice." In *A Companion to Late Antiquity*. Edited by Philip Rousseau, 377–91. Malden, MA: Wiley-Blackwell, 2009.

Humphreys, M.T.G. *Law, Power, and Imperial Ideology in the Iconoclast Era: c.680–850*. Oxford: Oxford University Press, 2015.

Jeffreys, Elizabeth. "Rhetoric." In *The Oxford Handbook of Byzantine Studies*. Edited by Elizabeth Jeffries, John F. Haldon, and Robin Cormack, 827–37. Oxford: Oxford University Press, 2008.

———. "Rhetoric in Byzantium." In *Companion to Greek Rhetoric*. Edited by Ian Worthington, 166–84. Malden, MA: Wiley-Blackwell, 2010.

Jeffreys, Michael and Marc D. Lauxtermann, eds. *The Letters of Psellos: Cultural Networks and Historical Realities*. Oxford: Oxford University Press, 2017.

Jordan, Robert, trans. *The Synaxrion of the Monastery of Theotokos Evergetis: March – August, The Moveable Cycle.* Belfast: Byzantine Enterprises, the Institute of Byzantine Studies, the Queen's University of Belfast, 2005.

Kaldellis, Anthony. "The Discontinuous History of Imperial Panegyric in Byzantium and its Reinvention by Michael Psellos." *Greek, Roman, and Byzantine Studies* 59 (2019): 693–713.

Karpozelos, A. "Realia in Byzantine Epistolography X–XIIc." *Byzantinische Zeitschrift* 77, no. 1 (1984): 20–37.

———. "Realia in Byzantine Epistolography XIII–XVc." *Byzantinische Zeitschrift* 88, no. 1 (1995): 68–84.

Kelly, Christopher. *Ruling the Later Roman Empire.* Cambridge, MA: Harvard University Press, 2004.

Kotsifu, Chrysi. "Monks as Mediators in Christian Egypt." In *Law and Legal Practice in Egypt from Alexander to the Arab Conquest.* Edited by James G. Keenan, J.G. Manning, and Uri Yiftach-Firanko, 530–40. Cambridge: Cambridge University Press, 2014.

Kustas, George L. *Studies in Byzantine Rhetoric.* Thessaloniki, 1973.

Layton, Bentley. *The Canons of Our Fathers: Monastic Rules of Shenoute.* Oxford: Oxford University Press, 2014.

———. "Social Structure and Food Consumption in an Early Christian Monastery: The Evidence of Shenoute's *Canons* and the White Monastery Federation," *Le Muséon* 115 (2002): 25–55.

Lenski, Noel E. "Evidence for the *Audienta episcopalis* in the New Letters of Augustine." In *Law, Society and Authority in Late Antiquity.* Edited by Ralph W. Mathisen, 83–97. Oxford: Oxford University Press, 2001.

Lieu, Samuel N.C., ed. *The Emperor Julian: Panegyric and Polemic: Claudius Mamertinus, John Chrysostom, Ephrem the Syrian.* Liverpool: Liverpool University Press, 1986.

Littlewood, A.R. "An 'Ikon of the Soul': The Byzantine Letter." *Visible Language* 10, no. 3 (1976): 197–226.

Lokin, J.H.A. "The Significance of Law and Legislation in the Law Books of the Ninth to Eleventh Centuries." In *Law and Society in Byzantium, Ninth-Twelfth Centuries.* Edited by Angeliki E. Laiou and Dieter Simon, 71–91. Washington, DC: Dumbarton Oaks Research Library and Collection, 1994.

MacCormack, Sabine G. *Art and Ceremony in Late Antiquity.* Berkeley: University of California, Press, 1981.

Malherbe, Abraham J. *Ancient Epistolary Theorists.* Atlanta, GA: Scholars Press, 1988.

Mango, Cyril, ed. and trans. *The Correspondence of Ignatios the Deacon: Text, Translation, and Commentary* by Cyril Mango, with the collaboration of Stephanos Efthymiadis. Washington DC: Dumbarton Oaks Research Library and Collection, 1997.

———. *The Homilies of Photius Patriarch of Constantinople, English Translation, Introduction and Commentary.* Cambridge, MA: Harvard University Press, 1958.

Marinis, Vasileios. "The *Vita of St. Anna/Euphemianos.* Introduction, Translation, and Commentary." *Journal of Modern Hellenism* 27–28 (2009–2010): 53–69.

Matthews John. *Laying Down the Law: A Study of the Theodosian Code.* New Haven: Yale University Press. 2000.

———. "The Making of the Text." In *The Theodosian Code: Studies in the Imperial Law of Late Antiquity.* Edited by Jill Harries and Ian Wood, 19–44. Ithaca, NY: Cornell University Press, 1993.

Meredith, Anthony. "Porphyry and Julian Against the Christians." *Aufstieg und Niedergang der römischen Welt* II. 23.2: 1119–49.

Miller, Patricia Cox. "Strategies of Representation in Collective Biography: Constructing the Subject as Holy." In *Greek Biography and Panegyric in Late Antiquity*. Edited by Tomas Hägg and Philip Rousseau, 209–54. Berkeley: University of California Press, 2000. (See also Patricia Cox)

Mullett, Margaret. "The Classical Tradition in the Byzantine Letter." In *Byzantium and the Classical Tradition*. Edited by Margaret Mullet and Roger Scott, 75–93. Birmingham: Centre for Byzantine Studies, 1981. Reprint, *Letters, Literacy and Literature in Byzantium*. Aldershot, UK/Burlington, VT: Ashgate, 2007.

———. "Epistolography." In *The Oxford Handbook of Byzantine Studies*. Edited by Elizabeth Jeffries, John F. Haldon, and Robin Cormack, 882–93. Oxford: Oxford University Press, 2008.

———. *Theophylact of Ochrid: Reading the Letters of a Byzantine Archbishop*. Aldershot, UK: Variorum, 1997.

———. "Writing in Early Medieval Byzantium." In *The Uses of Literacy in Early Medieval Europe*. Edited by R. McKitterick, 156–85. Cambridge, UK: Cambridge University Press, 1989. Reprint, *Letters, Literacy and Literature in Byzantium*. Aldershot, UK/Burlington, VT: Ashgate, 2007.

Nixon, C.E.V. "Constantinus Oriens Imperator: Propaganda and Panegyric. On Reading Panegyric 7 (307)." *Historia: Zeitschrift für Alte Geschichte* 42, no. 2 (1993): 229–46.

———. "Latin Panegyric in the Tetrarchic and Constantinian

Period." In *Latin Panegyric*. Edited by Roger Rees, 223–39. Oxford: Oxford University Press, 2012.

———. "*Panegyric of Constantine* by an Anonymous Orator (310)." In *In Praise of Later Roman Emperors: The Panegyrici Latini. Introduction, Translation and Historical Commentary*. Edited by C.E.V. Nixon and Barbara Saylor Rodgers, 211–53. Berkeley: University of California Press, 1994.

Nixon, C.E.V. and Barbara Saylor Rodgers. "General Introduction." In *In Praise of Later Roman Emperors: The Panegyrici Latini. Introduction, Translation and Historical Commentary*. Edited by C.E.V. Nixon and Barbara Saylor Rodgers, 1–37. Berkeley: University of California Press, 1994.

Paschalidis, Symeon A. "The Hagiography of the Eleventh and Twelfth Centuries." In *Ashgate Research Companion to Byzantine Hagiography*. Vol. 1, *Periods and Places*. Edited by Stephanos Efthymiadis, 143–71. Farnham/Burlington, VT: Ashgate, 2011.

Pernot, Laurent. *Epideictic Rhetoric: Questioning the Stakes of Ancient Praise*. Austin, TX: University of Texas Press, 2015.

Pellegrino, Michele. "General Introduction." In *Augustine. Sermons I (1–19)*. Translated by Michele Pellegrino. Edited by John E. Rotelle, 13–137. New York: New City Press, 2003.

Rees, Roger. *Layers of Loyalty in Latin Panegyric, AD 289–307*. Oxford: Oxford University Press, 2002.

———. "The Modern History of Latin Panegyric." In *Latin Panegyric*. Edited by Roger Rees, 3–48. Oxford: Oxford University Press, 2012.

Robinson, Diana. *Food, Virtue, and the Shaping of Early Christianity*. Cambridge, UK: Cambridge University Press, 2020.

Ross, Alan J. "Libanius the Historian? Praise and Presentation of the Past in *Or.* 59." *Greek, Roman, and Byzantine Studies* 56 (2016): 293-320.

Russell, D.A. and N.G. Wilson. *Menander Rhetor.* Edited with Translation and Commentary. Oxford: Oxford University Press, 1981.

Salzman, Michele Renee. "Introduction." In *The Letters of Symmachus: Book 1.* Translation by Michele Renee Salzman and Michael Roberts, with General Introduction and Commentary by Michele Renee Salzman, xiii–lxviii. Atlanta: Society of Biblical Literature, 2011.

———. "Travel and Communication in *The Letters of Symmachus.*" In *Travel, Communication and Geography in Late Antiquity: Sacred and Profane.* Edited by Linda Ellis and Frank L. Kidner, 81–94. Aldershot, UK/Burlington, VT: Ashgate Publishing, 2004. Reprint, New York: Routledge, 2016.

Scourfield, J.H.D. "Towards a Genre of Consolation." In *Greek and Roman Consolations: Eight Studies of a Tradition and Afterlife.* Edited by Han Baltussen, 1–36. Swansea: Classical Press of Wales, 2013.

Simon, Dieter. "Legislation as Both a World Order and a Legal Order." In *Law and Society in Byzantium, Ninth-Twelfth Centuries.* Edited by Angeliki E. Laiou and Dieter Simon, 1–25. Washington, DC: Dumbarton Oaks Research Library and Collection, 1994.

Schmelz, Georg. "Clerics as Arbiters in Christian Egypt." In *Law and Legal Practice in Egypt from Alexander to the Arab Conquest.* Edited by James G. Keenan, J.G. Manning, and Uri Yiftach-Firanko, 517–29. Cambridge, UK: Cambridge University Press, 2014.

Stolte, Bernard. "Justice: Legal Literature." In *The Oxford Handbook of Byzantine Studies*. Edited by Elizabeth Jeffries, John F. Haldon, and Robin Cormack, 691–98. Oxford: Oxford University Press, 2008.

Swain, Simon. *Themistius, Julian, and Greek Political Theory under Rome*: *Texts, Translations, and Studies of Four Key Works*. Cambridge, UK: Cambridge University Press, 2013.

Talbot, Alice-Mary. "General Introduction." In *Holy Women of Byzantium*: *Ten Saints' Lives in English Translation*. Edited by Alice-Mary Talbot, vii–xvi. Washington, DC: Dumbarton Oaks Research Library and Collection, 1996.

———. "Hagiography." In *The Oxford Handbook of Byzantine Studies*. Edited by Elizabeth Jeffries, John F. Haldon, and Robin Cormack, 862–71. Oxford: Oxford University Press, 2008.

Thomas, John and Angela Constantinides, eds., with the assistance of Giles Constable. *Byzantine Monastic Foundation Documents*: *A Complete Translations of the Surviving Founders' Typika and Testaments*. Vol. 1. Washington, DC: Dumbarton Oaks Research Library and Collection, 2000.

Tougher, Shaun. "In Praise of an Empress: Julian's *Speech of Thanks* to Eusebia." In *The Propaganda of Power*: *The Role of Panegyric in Late Antiquity*. Edited by Mary Whitby, 105–23. Leiden: Brill, 1998.

Tsironis, Niki. "Historicity and Poetry in Ninth-Century Homiletics: The Homilies of Patriarch Photios and George of Nicomedia." In *Preacher and Audience*: *Studies in Early Christian and Byzantine Homiletics*. Edited by Mary B. Cunningham and Pauline Allen, 295–315. Leiden: Brill, 1998.

Turner, H. J. M., ed. and trans. *The Epistles of St Symeon the New Theologian*. Edited with an Introduction, Translation, and Notes. Oxford: Oxford University Press, 2009.

Warmington, Brian. "Aspects of Constantinian Propaganda in the *Panegyrici Latini*." In *Latin Panegyric*. Edited by Roger Rees, 335–48. Oxford: Oxford University Press, 2012.

White, Carolinne. *The Correspondence (394–419) between Jerome and Augustine of Hippo*. New York: Edwin Mellen Press 1990.

———. *Lives of Roman Christian Women*. Translated and Edited with an Introduction and Notes. London, UK: Penguin, 2010.

Wilfong, T.G. *Women of Jeme: Lives in a Coptic Town in Late Antique Egypt*. Ann Arbor, MI: University of Michigan Press, 2002.

Worthington, Ian. *Companion to Greek Rhetoric*. Malden, MA: Wiley-Blackwell, 2010.

www.ingramcontent.com/pod-product-compliance
Lightning Source LLC
Chambersburg PA
CBHW060158050426
42446CB00013B/2889